Richard
Jefferies'
London

The Little Cloisters
Westminster Abbey

Richard Jefferies' London

EDITED
WITH AN INTRODUCTION AND NOTES
by

Samuel J. Looker

Illustrations specially drawn by
E. E. BRISCOE

Lutterworth Press
London and Redhill

Printed in Great Britain by
The Camelot Press Ltd., London and Southampton

To

Caroline Looker

The Good Companion
in London and Elsewhere

Contents

Illustrations

Introduction

I

RICHARD JEFFERIES WAS A SON OF THE SOIL, AND in all his writing his complete harmony with the spirit of the earth is revealed. He discovered the hidden ways of Nature and portrays with his pen all that he has seen in her lanes and byways, in the woods, on the hills, or by the sea. He appreciates the strange chances and changes experienced by the folk who are close to the essential life of the earth, the farmer, the village labourer, the gamekeeper and the poacher. He listens to the music of Nature and he receives; he loves and therefore he understands.

But Jefferies' power lay even deeper than this. His was the gift of imparting to others the spirit of place, and his prose brings to us in a vital way the natural background of our lives. It intensifies interest in and understanding of living creatures; it quickens delight in bird song; it illustrates the magic and influence of green leaf and coloured flower and becomes a part of the pleasure of all the myriad "sounds and sweet airs" that haunt the earth. It makes us increasingly aware of the splendour and benediction of the changing aspects of the sky over the well-loved downs and woodlands, and we become conscious, in a new way, of the wistful music of the waves which wash the English coast.

This power of understanding and its communication has placed Jefferies high among Nature writers and interpreters of the English countryside, but it is by no means so generally realized how great a part London plays in his writings. In the midst of his Nature studies, he was clearly conscious of the appeal of the great city, and these passages on London, collected from his writings and put together in this book, are convincing, I think, of his deep and abiding interest in London life. They show too, a profound understanding of the spirit of London, based upon his close and loving observation of people and places, and these are supplemented by the sketches and studies dealing with natural history near London. Their manner is as delightful as their matter, and not the least fascinating among them are those touched by the curious period spirit, the authentic Victorian atmosphere, such as "The Lions in Trafalgar Square," "Fleet Street," from "Amaryllis at the Fair," or "A Wet Night in London." Jefferies' thoughtful, gentle prose has not only a delicate and sweet music, but it is also full of interesting information and is stimulating to the mind.

Consider Jefferies' essay on "The Modern Thames," which is so accurate and lively. None of the great cities of the world is found without its patron river. How vital in London history has been the influence of our own great waterway, "the sweet Thames". But does not flowing water generally, and especially the presence of a mighty tidal river running through the heart of London with all its passionate, historic memories, bring Nature to our very doors? A. H. Sidgwick's comment on London's river, in his delightful essay "Walking Alone," published in 1912, is very pertinent:

> *The best gift of the river to London is simply itself, the long curving line on which the whole town is based, which links Fulham to Westminster and Battersea to the Docks.*

Above all, we must learn the lesson, as part of the spell of London and the attraction of its streets and houses, that much is due to the background of Nature. Londoners especially are great lovers of flowers, and a part of the charm of their leisure life, in the parks, gardens and elsewhere, is due to flowers, trees and birds—it was the great W. H. Hudson himself who wrote a book on "The Birds of London"—and we must think too, of the wonderful, if somewhat fugitive, glimpses of the sky above the crowded, busy streets. How often, on my homeward way through London's streets at evening, I have seen the stars quietly shining, calm and serene, above Fleet Street, or the moon, pale and beautiful, "the fair Immortal", on her endless journey.

Dr. Samuel Johnson liked London for another reason. Boswell reported that he said, "Sir, the chief advantage of London is, that a man is always so near his burrow."

It was Dr. Johnson, too, who thought that the full tide of human existence could be seen at Charing Cross, and who retorted to a critic, "No, Sir, when a man is tired of London, he is tired of life; for there is in London all that life can afford." Even the insular American sage and philosopher Emerson, in his "English Traits," was fain to admit the appeal, for he said: "London is the epitome of our time, and the Rome of to-day."

A typical passage, a charming and effective one, of Jefferies' attitude towards London and the spell it threw upon him, may be found in the essay entitled "Footpaths," collected in "Nature Near London," the first extract in this book.

Mirrored in Jefferies' pellucid prose is the affection that all true lovers of London must feel, as they experience the charm and fascination of wandering in the crowded, variegated streets of the vast city, until the very spirit of London enters the blood. For London has a soul, and the true Londoner, whether by birth or by adoption, is at one with it and understands his city as strangers can never do.

Such love and understanding is deepened and intensified by the tragic happenings of recent years, and the desolating destruction of much of the historic past.

Yes! It will be something gained if the study of Jefferies' London prose makes us recollect that kindly and prodigal Nature is still the background of man's life, even in his greatest cities, and how much all Londoners owe in rest of heart and refreshment of mind, in the midst of brick and stone, to the wind, the trees, the grass, the flowers, and the sky.

II

Richard Jefferies was born in 1848 at Coate Farm, in the hamlet of Coate, near Swindon, North Wiltshire. He came of old Wiltshire yeoman stock. His father was James Luckett Jefferies, his mother Elizabeth Gyde, of the Gydes of Painswick, Gloucestershire, also farming folk. James Luckett Jefferies, who farmed Coate Farm of some forty acres, was described by his son in "Amaryllis at the Fair" as Farmer Iden. James Luckett was a mixture of conflicting qualities and impulses, not a well-integrated personality, and somewhat intractable. He had some natural talents, with much knowledge of open-air life and lore, combined with an absence of any practical capacity to apply it. Still, Richard owed much to his father, who taught him a great deal about the countryside, especially animals, birds and trees, and something to his uncle, Thomas Harrild, who had married the sister of Elizabeth Gyde, and who was a letterpress and lithographic printer off Fleet Street. From both he gained much that he was to turn to good effect in his later writings and in his best novels.

Jefferies' mind was deeply coloured, all his life, by love of the country around Coate, the kind of country indeed, most likely to appeal to a boy of his meditative and introspective temper. For the first seventeen years of his life he lived quietly at home. He received a desultory education, but he supplemented this by wide and omnivorous reading. His real education, in fact, was the study of the life of the fields. It might have been said of him, with more truth than of the "Farmer's Boy", that "the fields were his study, nature was his book". As one who knew him well remarked, "With his unbending independence and self-centred judgment, Jefferies had no intimate confidences except with wild nature, his books, and his own soul."

At seventeen he became a newspaper reporter on the *North Wilts Herald*. These were difficult days. Jefferies had not as yet found his true medium of expression. He aspired to write fiction, which he thought a short cut to fame and fortune. His early efforts in that genre were crude, and "literary" in the worst sense. Fortunately, he soon found that his real strength lay elsewhere and began to write Nature essays based on what he had seen and felt in the life around him.

In 1874 Jefferies married a local farmer's daughter, Miss Jessie Baden. They had three children, one of whom died in infancy. In 1877 he removed from Wiltshire to Surbiton, to be near London and the opportunities life there would give him of keeping in touch with editors and publishers, as well as access to the Reading Room of the British Museum. At Surbiton he spent five productive writing years. His name had been brought before the public in November 1872, on the publication of a long letter to *The Times* on the condition of the Wiltshire agricultural labourer. Henceforward he was able to earn a living—a somewhat precarious and difficult one, it is true—by writing articles and essays on country and agricultural topics generally, for a variety of magazines and monthly reviews. Most of these essays were collected and published in volume form from time to time, but some still remain in manuscript.

Worn out by incessant mental labour and anxiety, and never very strong, Jefferies fell into a decline of health in 1882 and, after five years of suffering, during which he wrote much of his finest and most enduring work, died at Goring-on-Sea, near Worthing, at the early age of thirty-nine. He had lived in the meanwhile, after his removal from Surbiton, at Hove, Eltham and Crowborough.

The fame of Richard Jefferies has grown steadily since his death and his sincere, limpid and informative prose wins fresh admirers every year. On May 13th, 1939, a tablet of indication and remembrance was unveiled on Jefferies' House, Goring-on-Sea, by the Sussex novelist, Miss Sheila Kaye-Smith.

III

During his lifetime Richard Jefferies was a lonely and neglected figure. Shy and reserved by nature, and solitary in his habits, almost a recluse, he did not make friends easily, and there are but few personal memories of the man, and hardly any letters extant. He was poor all his life and, during the last few years, a very sick man. His life was heroic, and in the circumstances the general body of his work forms a truly remarkable and outstanding achievement.

As an interpreter of Nature there is no writer to take the place of Richard Jefferies and, although he has had many imitators, none can approach his level. W. H. Hudson is his only serious rival as an observer of wild life, but his work is so different in temper from that of Jefferies that it offers no real standard of comparison.

Jefferies is perhaps best studied at first in his earlier and simpler Nature books, such as "The Gamekeeper at Home", "The Amateur Poacher", "Roundabout a Great Estate", and "Wild Life in a Southern County". The strange, moving autobiography of his mind and thought, "The Story of My Heart", is far too esoteric for the generality, and has done his reputation no good service in a thoughtless and conventional world. Jefferies was too artless and sincere to take to heart the wise lines of William Blake,

> *Never seek to tell thy love,*
> *Love that never told can be.*

The selections included in this book are all taken from his later volumes of miscellaneous Nature essays, with the three exceptions of "The Story of My Heart", "Amaryllis at the Fair", and "After London". They may be said to rank among the most mature, illuminative and eloquent of his writings. They possess an ecstasy which is rare and delightful. His deep understanding of the lives of animals and birds may be seen even in such London essays as that of "The Pigeons at the British Museum". Like John Keats, Richard Jefferies could be at one with the very sparrow who pecks about the gravel.

IV

It was in February 1877 that Richard Jefferies removed his small household from Swindon to No. 2, Woodside, Surbiton. This was a two-storied house on the Ewell Road, on the way to Tolworth. From his front windows on one side, Jefferies would have a view, a far-reaching and wooded view, over Hounslow, Richmond Park and Wimbledon, and from the other side, he could see the woods of Hook, Chessington and Claygate. It is true that before this time Jefferies had spent holidays with his relations, the Harrilds, at Sydenham, but now in reality the spirit of London drew him, made him its own for the first time, and inspired some of his most trenchant and successful writing. He became powerfully conscious of the influence of the great city, an influence made even greater by the contrast of the Nature at his doors, which, so different from the downs and woods of his native Wiltshire, drew him, to use his own phrase, like a magnet, "the unseen influence of mighty London".

To the feeling for form and colour in Nature, Jefferies now united an interest in the varied, ever-changing scene of the London streets as he went to and fro on his journeys of exploration and business; his business often being that of meditation among the crowds, where he said he could think as long and as well as in the fields or woods. Richard Jefferies called himself "a student" not only of "nature, but of human life" also. Here, in the year 1877, at the age of twenty-nine, he was to find in this Surbiton period very great value in his development as a writer. These new London experiences quickened and shaped his imagination. He began to ponder on the poetry to be found in great cities, amid congregations of houses and men. "Ah, beautiful human life, tears come into my eyes as I think of it!" As a result of these more human studies, a more profound humanity, a deeper tint of thought, came into his writing, and even the poetry of Nature was strengthened thereby. In a letter to his publisher, towards the end of his Surbiton residence, he wrote: "I want to express the deeper feelings with which observation of life-histories has filled me, and I assure you that I have as large a collection of these facts and incidents—the natural history of the heart—as I have ever written about birds and trees." With John Keats, to whose mind

Jefferies' bears some affinity, he too would partake of the
exultations, agonies, the strife of human hearts, and would
not live apart in an ivory tower with the worship of beauty
alone. Something of what Jefferies means by "life-histories,
the natural history of the heart", we may see in passages
of his own masterpiece, "The Story of My Heart", and in
the moving and human cameos to be found here and
there in his collections of Nature essays, such as "Bits of
Oak Bark", or "The Field-Play" in "The Life of the
Fields", "Golden Brown" or "One of the New Voters"
in "The Open Air", or, to come closer home still, the
striking London essays included in this volume.

Jefferies walked in northern Surrey regularly. As in
Wiltshire, he loved to repeat his walks, and he speaks in
one place of making an almost daily pilgrimage to an
aspen by a brook. This was certainly the Hogsmill River
near Tolworth Court Farm. He sculled a boat on the
Thames at Teddington and Molesey. In his essay,
"The Modern Thames", he is writing of Thames Ditton;
in "A London Trout", of the Hogsmill again. As well as
Claygate, Tolworth, Hook and the rest, he had Banstead
Downs, Esher Common, and Oxshott not far away.

In "The Coming of Summer", a beautiful piece of
descriptive prose and close observation, he is writing of
the countryside just outside his own door; the Ewell Road
and the copse and orchard of which he wrote so frequently
and so well in "Nature Near London". It is especially
valuable to have so detailed, so delightful a picture of tree,
flower and bird life, around London sixty years ago, and
this account may be supplemented by the study of bird-
life set down in "Flocks of Birds". All these places, of
course, were far more rural in Jefferies' day than they are
now and the motor car was still to seek them out. It was
possible to wander and brood in these lanes, within a bow-

B

shot of the metropolis, where now suburban villas and bungalows stretch in every direction. Jefferies, a great lover of the sky in all its moods, who has written about it more lovingly and more perceptively than any writer since Ruskin, found the Thames Valley full of interest in his cloud studies; witness such passages as the exceptionally fine descriptions in "Magpie Fields" and elsewhere. Altogether, the Surbiton days were some of the most productive of his life and added their valuable quota to his experiences, inasmuch as for the first time he was in contact with all the stimulating influences of the greatest city in the world,

Now the heart of the world is in London, and the cities with the simulacrum of man in them are empty. They are moving images only; stand here, and you are real.

v

Arnold Bennett, in an entry in his journal, remarked that he could think best when he was in a street of shops and that he liked more and more looking at shop windows. Bennett, urbane man of the world, was far more of a townsman than Jefferies could ever be, but Jefferies too began to feel something of London's extraordinary power over the thinking man. Contact with crowds, shops, wandering in the London streets, the myriad carts, horses, carriages, and all the varied pageant of Cheapside or Trafalgar Square, acted as a stimulant to creative imagination. In "Sunlight in a London Square" and "Pigeons at the British Museum" he becomes lyrical over the beauty of London sunlight. There he saw "heaven brooding and descending in pure light upon man's handiwork". "Venice in the East End", an unforgettable painting of shipping at

the Docks, is of similar quality. "Red Roofs of London",
attractive and picturesque enough, is slighter in texture,
and less eloquent. It was written when Jefferies was living
at Eltham, under the influence of his journeys to London
Bridge by the London, Chatham and Dover Railway,
where the red-tiled Bermondsey roofs colour the approach.
"Herbs", his study written at Kew Gardens, is very
gracious in tone and is a fine piece of sustained descriptive
writing. Three essays, "A Wet Night in London", "On
the London Road", and "The Lions in Trafalgar Square",
are not the least interesting for the modern reader, for
they are pure period pieces and convey the flavour and
tone of a vanished age; the late mid-Victorian scene. Did
Jefferies know that here he was writing for posterity?
"Fleet Street" and the portrait of Alere Flamma, the
Bohemian artist, shows how powerfully "The Street of
Ink" had seized Jefferies' imagination: "Let the grandees
go to the opera, for me the streets", he writes in one place,
and in another: "Let the meads be never so sweet, the
mountain-top never so exalted, still to Fleet Street the
mind will return". Even in an earlier and less effective
novel than "Amaryllis at the Fair", "World's End",
published ten years before, Jefferies had thus described his
character Aymer Malet: "Like all men with any pretence
to brains, though he delighted in Nature and loved the
country, there was a strong, almost irresistible desire
within him to mingle in the vast crowd of cities, to feel
that indefinable 'life' which animates the mass." If Jefferies
himself kept aloof, apart from intimate friendship and
communication, it was, we may be sure, due to no lack
of love or sympathy for the life of his time, but an attempt,
as an observer and commentator, to preserve his independence and originality. The view of Frederick
Greenwood, the famous editor, who knew him well, was,

that "Jefferies deliberately shunned society to avoid losing his native sensibility".

The selection from "After London", or "Wild England", Richard Jefferies' sombre picture of a dead civilization, is a kind of ironical postscript. Here, with real power and a greater show of the inventive faculty than he usually displays, he describes "the relapse of England into barbarism, and the loss of everything characteristic of the Nineteenth Century".

Not only by reason of its originality, "After London" takes a high place in the Jefferies' canon. It is a successful example of a form of writing in a difficult genre, which can be made very tiresome in unskilled or too didactic hands.

Not even Macaulay's famous "New Zealander", musing amid the ruins of London Bridge, is a more striking figure than Felix Aquila as, lost and mad for fresh water, he wanders in the pestilent and dreadful swamps, where all is "black water, red mud and yellow vapour, the very essence of corruption". Nor can anything be more terrible than his plight when, with drugged mind and numbed limbs, shuddering with horror, he realizes that the deserted and utterly extinct city of London lies under his feet. Edward Thomas thought with justice that it was one of Jefferies' masterpieces in description.

VI

The face of London has changed since Jefferies' day, but its spirit still remains. Many one-time famous landmarks in the City and West End have given place to modern buildings; horse-driven carts and carriages have been replaced by the lorry and the motor car; even the fog—that heavy scourge of my youth, "the London

Particular"—has to a certain extent been countered by the increasing use of electricity; and there is nothing now to parallel the inferno of the old steam-driven District Railway. Habits and clothes have changed too, very much for the better. Women have invaded the City and the West End since Jefferies' day and have brought fresh colour and a brisker air with them. Yet despite all this, in reading these London essays, it is surprising how clear and accurate they still seem. *The Spirit of London*, it is for this we read them, and that does not change!

The City of London, which stands in the centre of Greater London, covers only 675 acres—just over one square mile. It had a population of eleven thousand at the last census. The County of London covers 116 square miles and embraces five million people. Greater London, with a radius of fifteen miles from Charing Cross, has eight millions. The parks and open spaces alone of Greater London occupy 5056 acres. Although it has so much grown in extent since Jefferies' day, yet even then, Greater London was a vast and complex entity. The City itself, with Trafalgar Square and the British Museum, drew most of Jefferies' attention, and the atmosphere they have created has a way of subduing all around them to their own quality.

To one who has known Trafalgar Square through all vicissitudes for over forty years, the same spirit seems to brood over it. As one stands with Jefferies looking south-wards, towards the green trees, still the hum and roar of the great city rises to the ear, fearful and muted in the sunlight, while the nameless and unknown crowd of the pavements passes and repasses, in this spot which has been called the centre of the world.

Other great writers have felt this and have expressed the feeling in a memorable way. Thus Hallam Tennyson

in the life of his father says that Lord Tennyson always
delighted in the "central roar" of London. "Whenever
he and I", he continues, "went to London, one of the
first things we did was to walk to the Strand and Fleet
Street. 'Instead of the stuccoed houses in the West End,
this is the place where I should like to live,' he would say.
He was also fond of looking at London from the bridges
over the Thames, and of going into St. Paul's, and into
the Abbey. One day in 1842 Fitzgerald records a visit to
St. Paul's with him when he said, 'Merely as an enclosed
space in a huge city this is very fine,' and when they got
out into the open, in the midst of the 'central roar', 'This
is the mind; that is a mood of it.' "

I hope it will be thought that these distinctive London
Essays, and passages from Richard Jefferies' other writings
which bear on the same subject, never before collected,
are of great interest and value. Each in its degree has its
own special colour and plays its part in building up an
authentic picture of the time. The apotheosis of his London
experiences, however, is to be found in the magnificent
pages in "The Story of My Heart", where, as Jefferies
stands on the pavement before the Royal Exchange, he
watches the great pageant of moving human life before
him, or on London Bridge, where the sunrise over the
river reminds him of another and more unearthly splendour. Jefferies' acquaintance with London had opened his
mind, much more clearly than heretofore, to an interest
in civilization. "Nature", he writes, "was deepened by the
crowds and foot-worn stones." His sense of the past,
always strong, but hitherto rooted only in imagination,
was made real. Standing in Trafalgar Square, looking at
the passers-by, he thought of the people, "not as mere
buyers and sellers, as mere counters, but as human beings—
beings possessed of hearts and minds, full of the passions

and the hopes and fears which made the ancient poets great merely to record. These are the same passions that were felt in antique Rome, whose very name is a section of human life. *There is colour in these lives now as then*". This is the essence of Jefferies' London teaching.

Jefferies has a simple pathos at all times, for he felt deeply and was powerfully moved by his emotions to the creation of beauty in words, and he has the rare gift of making this beauty real to others. But now these talents, which had served him so well in the depiction of the English countryside, came to his aid when he wished to interpret a far different scene. With deep feeling, yet with the sharp observant eye of the artist, he communicates the *Spirit of London*.

SAMUEL J. LOOKER.

BILLERICAY, ESSEX.

London Overture

NEVER GO BY A STILE WITHOUT GETTING OVER IT and following the path. But they all end in one place. After rambling across furze and heath, or through dark fir woods; after lingering in the meadows among the buttercups, or by the copses where the pheasants crow; after gathering June roses, or in later days staining the lips with blackberries, or cracking nuts, by and by the path brings you in sight of a railway station. And the railway station, through some process of mind, presently compels you to go up on the platform, and after a little puffing and revolution of wheels, you emerge at Charing Cross, or London Bridge, or Waterloo, or Ludgate Hill, and with the freshness of the meadows still clinging to your coat, mingle with the crowd. The inevitable end of every footpath roundabout London, is London. All paths go thither. If it were far away in the distant country you might sit down in the shadow upon the hay and fall asleep, or dream awake, hour after hour. There would be no inclination to move. But if you sat down on the grass, under the ancient pollard oak in the little mead with the brook and the wood of which I spoke just now as like a glade in the enchanted forest of Arden, this would not be possible. It is the proximity of the immense city which induces a mental, a nerve restlessness. As you sit and would dream, a something plucks at the mind with constant reminder; you cannot dream for long, you must up, and away, and, turn in which direction you please, ultimately it will lead you to London.

There is a fascination in it, there is a magnetism stronger than that of the rock which drew the nails from Sinbad's ship. You are like a bird let out with a string tied to the foot to flutter a little way and return again. It is not business, for you may have none, in the ordinary sense; it is not "society", it is not pleasure. It is the presence of man in his myriads. There is something in the heart which cannot be satisfied away from it. It is a curious thing that your nextdoor neighbour may be a stranger, but there are no strangers in a vast crowd. They all seem to have some relationship, or rather, perhaps, they do not rouse the sense of reserve which a single unknown person might. Still, the impulse is not to be analysed, these are mere notes acknowledging its power. The hills and vales, and meads and woods, are like the ocean on which Sinbad sailed; but coming to near the lodestone of London, the ship wends thither, whether or no.

At least it is so with me, and I often go to London without any object whatever, but just because I must, and, arriving there, wander whithersoever the hurrying throng carries me.

The Story of My Heart

I

I WAS MUCH IN LONDON, AND, ENGAGEMENTS COM-
pleted, I wandered about in the same way as in the
woods of former days. From the stone bridges I
looked down on the river; the gritty dust, straws that
lie on the bridges, flew up and whirled round with every
gust from the flowing tide; gritty dust that settles in the
nostrils and on the lips, the very residuum of all that is
repulsive in the greatest city of the world. The noise of
the traffic and the constant pressure from the crowds
passing, their incessant and disjointed talk, could not
distract me. One moment at least I had, a moment when
I thought of the push of the great sea forcing the water
to flow under the feet of these crowds, the distant sea
strong and splendid; when I saw the sunlight gleam on
the tidal wavelets; when I felt the wind and was conscious of the earth, the sea, the sun, the air, the immense
forces working on, while the city hummed by the river.
Nature was deepened by the crowds and foot-worn stones.
If the tide had ebbed, and the masts of the vessels were
tilted as the hulls rested on the shelving mud, still even
the blackened mud did not prevent my seeing the water
as water flowing to the sea. The sea had drawn down,
and the wavelets washing the strand here as they hastened
were running the faster to it. Eastwards from London
Bridge the river raced to the ocean.

The bright morning sun of summer heated the eastern
parapet of London Bridge; I stayed in the recess to
acknowledge it. The smooth water was a broad sheen of

light, the built-up river flowed calm and silent by a thousand doors, rippling only where the stream chafed against a chain. Red pennants drooped, gilded vanes gleamed on polished masts, black-pitched hulls glistened like a black rook's feathers in sunlight; the clear air cut out the forward angles of the warehouses, the shadowed wharves were quiet in shadows that carried light; far down the ships that were hauling out moved in repose, and with the stream floated away into the summer mist. There was a faint blue colour in the air hovering between the built-up banks, against the lit walls, in the hollows of the houses. The swallows wheeled and climbed, twittered and glided downwards. Burning on, the great sun stood in the sky, heating the parapet, glowing steadfastly upon me as when I rested in the narrow valley grooved out in prehistoric times. Burning on steadfast, and ever present as my thought. Lighting the broad river, the broad walls; lighting the least speck of dust; lighting the great heaven; gleaming on my finger-nail. The fixed point of day—the sun. I was intensely conscious of it; I felt it; I felt the presence of the immense powers of the universe; I felt out into the depths of the ether. So intensely conscious of the sun, the sky, the limitless space, I felt too in the midst of eternity then, in the midst of the supernatural, among the immortal, and the greatness of the material realized the spirit. By these I saw my soul; by these I knew the supernatural to be more intensely real than the sun. I touched the supernatural, the immortal, there that moment.

When, weary of walking on the pavements, I went to rest in the National Gallery, I sat and rested before one or other of the human pictures. I am not a picture lover, they are flat surfaces, but those that I call human are nevertheless beautiful. The knee in Daphnis and Chloe and the breast are like living things; they draw the heart towards them, the heart must love them . . . I lived in looking; without beauty there is no life for me, the divine beauty of flesh is life itself to me. The shoulder in the Surprise, the rounded rise of the bust, the exquisite tints of the ripe skin, momentarily gratified the sea-thirst in me. For I thirst with all the thirst of the salt sea, and the sun-heated sands dry for the tide, with all the sea I thirst for beauty. And I know full well that one lifetime, how-ever long, cannot fill my heart. My throat and tongue and whole body have often been parched and feverish dry with this measureless thirst, and again moist to the fingers' ends like a sappy bough. It burns in me as the sun burns in the sky.

The glowing face of Cytherea in Titian's Venus and Adonis, the heated cheek, the lips that kiss each eye that gazes on them, the desiring glance, the golden hair—sunbeams moulded into features—this face answered me. Juno's wide back and mesial groove, is anything so lovely as the back? Cytherea's poised hips unveiled for judgment; these called up the same thirst I felt on the green sward in the sun, on the wild beach listening to the quiet sob as the summer wave drank at the land. I will search the world through for beauty. I came here and sat to rest before these in the days when I could not afford to buy so much as a glass of ale, weary and faint from walking on stone pavements. I came later on, in better times, often straight from labours which though necessary will ever be distasteful, always to rest my heart with loveli-ness. I go still; the divine beauty of flesh is life itself to me. It was, and is, one of my London pilgrimages.

Another was to the Greek sculpture galleries in the British Museum. The statues are not, it is said, the best; broken too, and mutilated, and seen in a dull, commonplace light. But they were shape—divine shape of man and woman; the form of limb and torso, of bust and neck, gave me a sighing sense of rest. These were they who would have stayed with me under the shadow of the oaks while the blackbirds fluted and the south air swung the cowslips. They would have walked with me among the reddened gold of the wheat. They would have rested with me on the hill-tops and in the narrow valley grooved of ancient times. They would have listened with me to the sob of the summer sea drinking the land. These had thirsted of sun, and earth, and sea, and sky. Their shape spoke this thirst and desire like mine—if I had lived with them from Greece till now I should not have had enough of them. Tracing the form of limb and torso with the eye gave me a sense of rest.

Sometimes I came in from the crowded streets and ceaseless hum; one glance at these shapes and I became myself. Sometimes I came from the Reading-room, where under the dome I often looked up from the desk and realized the crushing hopelessness of books, useless, not equal to one bubble borne along on the running brook I had walked by, giving no thought like the spring when I lifted the water in my hand and saw the light gleam on it. Torso and limb, bust and neck instantly returned me to myself; I felt as I did lying on the turf listening to the wind among the grass; it would have seemed natural to have found butterflies fluttering among the statues. The same deep desire was with me. I shall always go to speak to them; they are a place of pilgrimage; wherever there is a beautiful statue there is a place of pilgrimage.

II

There is a place in front of the Royal Exchange where the wide pavement reaches out like a promontory. It is

in the shape of a triangle with a rounded apex. A stream
of traffic runs on either side, and other streets send their
currents down into the open space before it. Like the
spokes of a wheel converging streams of human life flow
into this agitated pool. Horses and carriages, carts, vans,
omnibuses, cabs, every kind of conveyance cross each
other's course in every possible direction. Twisting in and
out by the wheels and under the horses' heads, working
a devious way, men and women of all conditions wind
a path over. They fill the interstices between the carriages
and blacken the surface, till the vans almost float on human
beings. Now the streams slacken, and now they rush
amain, but never cease; dark waves are always rolling
down the incline opposite, waves swell out from the side
rivers, all London converges into this focus. There is an
indistinguishable noise—it is not clatter, hum or roar, it
is not resolvable; made up of a thousand thousand footsteps, from a thousand hoofs, a thousand wheels—of
haste, and shuffle, and quick movements, and ponderous
loads; no attention can resolve it into a fixed sound.

Blue carts and yellow omnibuses, varnished carriages
and brown vans, green omnibuses and red cabs, pale loads
of yellow straw, rusty-red iron clanking on paintless carts,
high white woolpacks, grey horses, bay horses, black
teams; sunlight sparkling on brass harness, gleaming from
carriage panels; jingle, jingle, jingle! An intermixed and
intertangled, ceaselessly changing jingle, too, of colour;
flecks of colour champed, as it were, like bits in the horses'
teeth, frothed and strewn about, and a surface always of
dark-dressed people winding like the curves on fast-
flowing water. This is the vortex and whirlpool, the
centre of human life to-day on the earth. Now the tide
rises and now it sinks, but the flow of these rivers always
continues. Here it seethes and whirls, not for an hour only,

but for all present time, hour by hour, day by day, year by year.

Here it rushes and pushes, the atoms triturate and grind, and, eagerly thrusting by, pursue their separate ends. Here it appears in its unconcealed personality, indifferent to all else but itself, absorbed and rapt in eager self, devoid and stripped of conventional gloss and politeness, yielding only to get its own way; driving, pushing, carried on in a stress of feverish force like a bullet, dynamic force apart from reason or will, like the force that lifts the tides and sends the clouds onwards. The friction of a thousand interests evolves a condition of electricity in which men are moved to and fro without considering their steps. Yet the agitated pool of life is stonily indifferent, the thought is absent or preoccupied, for it is evident that the mass are unconscious of the scene in which they act.

But it is more sternly real than the very stones, for all these men and women that pass through are driven on by the push of accumulated circumstances; they cannot stay, they must go, their necks are in the slave's ring, they are beaten like seaweed against the solid walls of fact. In ancient times, Xerxes, the king of kings, looking down upon his myriads, wept to think that in a hundred years not one of them would be left. Where will be these millions of to-day in a hundred years? But, further than that, let us ask, where then will be the sum and outcome of their labour? If they wither away like summer grass, will not at least a result be left which those of a hundred years hence may be the better for? No, not one jot! There will not be any sum or outcome or result of this ceaseless labour and movement; it vanishes in the moment that it is done, and in a hundred years nothing will be there, for nothing is there now. There will be no more sum or result than accumulates from the motion of a revolving cowl on a housetop. Nor do they receive any more sunshine during their lives, for they are unconscious of the sun.

I used to come and stand near the apex of the promontory of pavement which juts out towards the pool of life; I still go there to ponder. Burning in the sky the sun shone on me as when I rested in the narrow valley carved in pre-historic times. Burning in the sky, I can never forget the sun. The heat of summer is dry there as if the light carried an impalpable dust; dry, breathless heat that will not let the skin respire, but swathes up the dry fire in the blood. But beyond the heat and light, I felt the presence of the sun as it felt in the solitary valley, the presence of the resistless forces of the universe; the sun burned in the sky as I stood and pondered. Is there any theory, philosophy, or creed, is there any system of culture, and formulated method able to meet and satisfy each separate item of this agitated pool of human life? By which they may be guided, by which hope, by which look forward? Not a mere illusion of the craving heart—something real, as real as the solid walls of fact against which, like drifted seaweed, they are dashed; something to give each separate per-sonality sunshine and a flower in its own existence now; something to shape this million-handed labour to an end and outcome that will leave more sunshine and more flowers to those who must succeed? Something real now, and not in the spirit-land; in this hour now, as I stand and the sun burns. Can any creed, philosophy, system, or culture endure the test and remain unmolten in this fierce focus of human life?

Consider, is there anything slowly painted on the once mystic and now commonplace papyri of ancient, ancient Egypt, held on the mummy's withered breast? In that elaborate ritual, in the procession of the symbols, in the winged circle, in the laborious sarcophagus? Nothing;

c

absolutely nothing! Before the fierce heat of the human furnace, the papyri smoulder away as paper smoulders under a lens in the sun. Remember Nineveh and the cult of the fir-cone, the turbaned and bearded bulls of stone, the lion hunt, the painted chambers loaded with tile books, the lore of the arrow-headed writing. What is in Assyria? There is sand, and failing rivers, and in Assyria's writings an utter nothing. The aged caves of India, who shall tell when they were sculptured? Far back when the sun was burning, burning in the sky as now in untold precedent time. Is there any meaning in those ancient caves? The indistinguishable noise not to be resolved, born of the human struggle, mocks in answer.

In the strange characters of the Zend, in the Sanscrit, in the effortless creed of Confucius, in the Aztec coloured-string writings and rayed stones, in the uncertain marks left of the sunken Polynesian continent, hieroglyphics as useless as those of Memphis, nothing. Nothing! They have been tried, and were found an illusion. Think then, to-day, now looking from this apex of the pavement promontory outwards from our own land to the utmost bounds of the farthest sail, is there any faith or culture at this hour which can stand in this fierce heat? From the various forms of Semitic, Aryan, or Turanian creed now existing, from the printing-press to the palm leaf volume on to those who call on the jewel in the lotus, can aught be gathered which can face this, the Reality? The indistinguishable noise, non-resolvable, roars a loud contempt.

Turn, then, to the calm reasoning of Aristotle; is there anything in that? Can the half-divine thought of Plato, rising in storeys of sequential ideas, following each other to the conclusion, endure here? No! All the philosophers in Diogenes Laertius fade away; the theories of mediaeval days; the organon of experiment; down to this hour—

they are useless alike. The science of this hour, drawn
from the printing-press in an endless web of paper, is
powerless here; the indistinguishable noise echoed from
the smoke-shadowed walls despises the whole. A thousand
footsteps, a thousand hoofs, a thousand wheels roll over
and utterly contemn them in complete annihilation. Mere
illusions of heart or mind, they are tested and thrust aside
by the irresistible push of a million converging feet.

Burning in the sky the sun shines as it shone on me in
the solitary valley, as it burned on when the earliest cave
of India was carved. Above the indistinguishable roar of
the many feet I feel the presence of the sun, of the immense
forces of the universe, and beyond these the sense of the
eternal now, of the immortal. Full well aware that all has
failed, yet, side by side with the sadness of that knowledge,
there lives on in me an unquenchable belief, thought burning like the sun, that there is yet something to be found,
something real, something to give each separate per-
sonality sunshine and flowers in its own existence now.
Something to shape this million-handed labour to an end
and outcome, leaving accumulated sunshine and flowers to
those who shall succeed. It must be dragged forth by might
of thought from the immense forces of the universe.

3

The Lions in Trafalgar Square

THE LIONS IN TRAFALGAR SQUARE ARE TO ME THE centre of London. By those lions began my London work; from them, as spokes from the middle of a wheel, radiate my London thoughts. Standing by them and looking south you have in front the Houses of Parliament, where resides the mastership of England; at your back is the National Gallery—that is art; and farther back the British Museum—books. To the right lies the wealth and luxury of the West End; to the left the roar and labour, the craft and gold, of the City. For themselves, they are the only monument in this vast capital worthy of a second visit as a monument. Over the entire area covered by the metropolis there does not exist another work of art in the open air. There are many structures and things, no other art.[1] The outlines of the great animals, the bold curves and firm touches of the master hand, the deep indents, as it were, of his thumb on the plastic metal, all the *technique* and grasp written there, is legible at a glance. Then comes the *pose* and expression of the whole, the calm strength in repose, the indifference to little things, the resolute view of great ones. Lastly, the soul of the maker, the spirit which was taken from nature, abides in the massive bronze. These lions are finer than those that crouch in the cages at the Zoological Gardens; these are truer and more real, and, besides, these are lions to whom has been added the heart of a man. Nothing disfigures them; smoke and, what is much worse, black

[1] This is altered since Jefferies wrote.

St. Martin's
Church,
Trafalgar Square

E.E.BRISCOE

rain—rain which washes the atmosphere of the suspended
mud—does not affect them in the least. If the choke-damp
of fog obscures them, it leaves no stain on the design; if
the surfaces be stained, the idea made tangible in metal is
not. They are no more touched than Time itself by the
alternations of the seasons. The only noble open-air work
of native art in the great city, they rest there supreme and
are the centre. Did such a work exist now in Venice, what
immense folios would be issued about it! All the language
of the studios would be huddled together in piled-up and
running-over laudation, and curses on our insular swine-
eyes that could not see it. I have not been to Venice,
therefore I do not pretend to a knowledge of that mediaeval
potsherd; this I do know, that in all the endless pictures
on the walls of the galleries in London, year after year
exposed and disappearing like snow somewhere unseen,
never has there appeared one with such a subject as this.
Weak, feeble, mosaic, gimcrack, coloured tiles, and far-
fetched compound monsters, artificial as the graining on
a deal front door, they cannot be compared; it is the
gingerbread gilt on a circus car to the column of a Greek
temple. This is pure open air, grand as Nature herself,
because it *is* Nature with, as I say, the heart of a man
added.

But if any one desire the meretricious painting of warm
light and cool yet not hard shade, the effect of colour,
with the twitching of triangles, the spangles glittering, and
all the arrangement contrived to take the eye, then he can
have it here as well as noble sculpture. Ascend the steps
to the National Gallery, and stand looking over the
balustrade down across the square in summer hours. Let
the sun have sloped enough to throw a slant of shadow
outward; let the fountains splash whose bubbles restless
speak of rest and leisure, idle and dreamy; let the blue-

tinted pigeons nod their heads walking, and anon crowd through the air to the roof-tops. Shadow upon the one side, bright light upon the other, azure above and swallows. Ever rolling the human stream flows, mostly on the south side yonder, near enough to be audible, but toned to bearableness. A stream of human hearts, every atom a living mind filled with what thoughts?—a stream that ran through Rome once, but has altered its course and wears away the banks here now and triturates its own atoms, the hearts, to dust in the process. Yellow omnibuses and red cabs, dark shining carriages, chestnut horses, all rushing, and by their motion mixing their colours so that the commonness of it disappears and the hues remain, a streak drawn in the groove of the street—dashed hastily with thick camel's hair. In the midst the calm lions, dusky, unmoved, full always of the one grand idea that was infused into them. So full of it that the golden sun and the bright wall of the eastern houses, the shade that is slipping towards them, the sweet swallows and the azure sky, all the human stream holds of wealth and power and coroneted panels—nature, man, and city—pass as naught. Mind is stronger than matter. The soul alone stands when the sun sinks, when the shade is universal night, when the van's wheels are silent and the dust rises no more.

At summer noontide, when the day surrounds us and it is bright light even in the shadow, I like to stand by one of the lions and yield to the old feeling. The sunshine glows on the dusky creature, as it seems, not on the surface, but under the skin, as if it came up from out of the limb. The roar of the rolling wheels sinks and becomes distant as the sound of a waterfall when dreams are coming. All the abundant human life is smoothed and levelled, the abruptness of the individuals lost in the flowing current, like separate flowers drawn along in a border,

like music heard so far off that the notes are molten and
the theme only remains. The abyss of the sky over and the
ancient sun are near. They only are close at hand, they
and immortal thought. When the yellow Syrian lions
stood in old time of Egypt, then, too, the sunlight gleamed
on the eyes of men, as now this hour on mine. The same
consciousness of light, the same sun, but the eyes that saw
it and mine, how far apart! The immense lion here beside me expresses larger nature-cosmos—the ever-existent
thought which sustains the world. Massiveness exalts the
mind till the vast roads of space which the sun tramples
are as an arm's-length. Such a moment cannot endure
long; gradually the roar deepens, the current resolves into
individuals, the houses return—it is only a square.

But a square potent. For London is the only *real* place
in the world. The cities turn towards London as young
partridges run to their mother. The cities know that they
are not real. They are only houses and wharves, and
bricks and stucco; only outside. The minds of all men in
them, merchants, artists, thinkers, are bent on London . . .
A house is not a dwelling if a man's heart be elsewhere.
Now, the heart of the world is in London, and the cities
with the simulacrum of man in them are empty. They
are moving images only; stand here and you are real.

4

Sky over London

THERE ARE OAKS ON VILLA LAWNS NEAR LONDON whose glory of russet foliage in October or November is not to be surpassed in the parks of the country. There are two or three such oaks in Long Ditton. All oaks do not become russet, or buff; some never take those tints. An oak, for instance, not far from those just mentioned, never quite loses its green; it cannot be said, indeed, to remain green, but there is a trace of it somewhere; the leaves must, I suppose, be partly buff and partly green; and the mixture of these colours in bright sunshine produces a tint for which I know no accurate term.

In the tops of the poplars, where most exposed, the leaves stay till the last, those growing on the trunk below disappearing long before those on the spire, which bends to every blast. The keys of the hornbeam come twirling down: the hornbeam and the beech are characteristic trees of the London landscape—the latter reaches a great height and never loses its beauty, for when devoid of leaves the feathery spray-like branches only come into view the more.

The abundant bird life is again demonstrated as the evening approaches. Along the hedgerows, at the corners of the copses, wherever there is the least cover, so soon as the sun sinks the blackbirds announce their presence by their calls. Their "ching, chinging" sounds everywhere; they come out on the projecting branches and cry, then fly fifty yards further down the hedge, and cry again. During the day they may not have been noticed, scattered as they were under the bushes, but the dusky shadows darkening the fields send them to roost, and before finally retiring they "ching-ching" to each other.

Then, almost immediately after the sun has gone down, looking to the south-west the sky seen above the trees (which hide the yellow sunset) becomes a delicate violet. Soon a speck of light gleams faintly through it—the merest speck. The first appearance of a star is very beautiful; the actual moment of first contact as it were of the ray with the eye is always a surprise, however often you may have enjoyed it, and notwithstanding that you are aware it will happen. Where there was only the indefinite violet before, the most intense gaze into which could discover nothing, suddenly, as if at that moment born, the point of light arrives.

So glorious is the night that not all London, with its glare and smoke, can smother the sky; in the midst of the gas, and the roar and the driving crowd, look up from the pavement, and there, straight above, are the calm stars. I never forget them, not even in the restless Strand; they face one coming down the hill of the Haymarket; in Trafalgar Square, looking towards the high dark structure of the House at Westminster, the clear bright steel silver of the planet Jupiter shines unwearied, without sparkle or flicker.

Apart from the grand atmospheric changes caused by a storm wave from the Atlantic, or an anti-cyclone, London produces its own sky. Put a shepherd on St. Paul's, allow him three months to get accustomed to the local appearances and the deceptive smoke clouds, and he would then tell what the weather of the day was going to be far more efficiently than the very best instrument ever yet invented. He would not always be right; but he would predict the local London weather with far more accuracy than any one reading the returns from the barometers at Valentia, Stornaway, Brest, or Christiansand.

The reason is this—the barometer foretells the cloud in the sky, but cannot tell where it will burst. The practised eye can judge with very considerable accuracy where the discharge will take place. Some idea of what the local weather of London will be for the next few hours may often be obtained by observation on any of the bridges—Westminster, Waterloo, or London Bridge: there is on the bridges something like a horizon, the best to be got in the City itself, and the changes announce themselves very clearly there. The difference in the definition is really wonderful.

From Waterloo Bridge the golden cross on St. Paul's and the dome at one time stand out as if engraved upon the sky, clear and with a white aspect. At the same time, the brick of the old buildings at the back of the Strand is red and bright. The structures of the bridges appear light, and do not press upon their arches. The yellow straw stacked on the barges is bright, the copper-tinted sails bright, the white wall of the Embankment clear, and the lions' heads distinct. Every trace of colour, in short, is visible.

At another time the dome is murky, the cross tarnished, the outline dim, the red brick dull, the whiteness gone. In summer there is occasionally a bluish haze about the distant buildings. These are the same changes presented by the Downs in the country, and betoken the state of the atmosphere as clearly. The London atmosphere is, I should fancy, quite as well adapted to the artist's uses as the changeless glare of the Continent. The smoke itself is not without its interest.

Sometimes upon Westminster Bridge at night the scene is very striking. Vast rugged columns of vapour rise up

St. Paul's
Cathedral
from Waterloo
Bridge

—E.E.BRISCOE—

behind and over the towers of the House, hanging with threatening aspect; westward the sky is nearly clear, with some relic of the sunset glow; the river itself, black or illuminated with the electric light, imparting a silvery blue tint, crossed again with the red lamps of the steamers. The aurora of dark vapour, streamers extending from the thicker masses, slowly moves and yet does not go away; it is just such a sky as a painter might give to some tremendous historical event, a sky big with presage, gloom, tragedy. How bright and clear, again, are the mornings in summer! I once watched the sun rise on London Bridge, and never forgot it.[1]

In frosty weather, again, when the houses take hard, stern tints, when the sky is clear over great part of its extent, but with heavy thunderous-looking clouds in places—clouds full of snow—the sun becomes of a red or orange hue, and reminds one of the lines of Longfellow when Othere reached the North Cape—

> *Round in a fiery ring*
> *Went the great sun, oh King!*
> *With red and lurid light.*

The redness of the winter sun in London is, indeed, characteristic.

A sunset in winter or early spring floods the streets with fiery glow. It comes, for instance, down Piccadilly; it is reflected from the smooth varnished roofs of the endless carriages that roll to and fro like the flicker of a mighty fire; it streaks the side of the street with rosiness. The faces of those who are passing are lit up by it, all unconscious as they are. The sky above London, indeed, is as full of interest as above the hills. Lunar rainbows occasionally occur; two to my knowledge were seen in

[1] This experience is described in "The Story of My Heart".

the direction and apparently over the metropolis recently.

When a few minutes on the rail has carried you outside the hub as it were of London, among the quiet tree-skirted villas, the night reigns as completely as in the solitudes of the country. Perhaps even more so, for the solitude is somehow more apparent. The last theatre-goer has disappeared inside his hall door, the last dull roll of the brougham, with its happy laughing load, has died away—there is not so much as a single footfall. The cropped holly hedges, the leafless birches, the limes and acacias are still and distinct in the moonlight. A few steps further out on the highway the copse or plantation sleeps in utter silence.

But the tall elms are the most striking; the length of the branches and their height above brings them across the light, so that they stand out even more shapely than when in leaf. The blue sky (not, of course, the blue of day), the white moonlight, the bright stars—larger at midnight and brilliant, in despite of the moon, which cannot over-power them in winter as she does in summer evenings—all are as beautiful as on the distant hills of old. By night, at least, even here, in the still silence, Heaven has her own way.

5

Sunlight in a London Square[1]

THERE ARE DAYS NOW AND AGAIN WHEN THE summer broods in Trafalgar Square; the flood of light from a cloudless sky gathers and grows, thickening the air; the houses enclose the beams as water is enclosed in a cup. Sideways from the white-painted walls light is reflected; upwards from the broad, heated pavement in the centre light and heat ascend; from the blue heaven it presses downwards. Not only from the sun— one point—but from the entire width of the visible blue the brilliant stream flows. Summer is enclosed between the banks of houses—all summer's glow and glory of exceeding brightness. The blue panel overhead has but a stray fleck of cloud, a Cupid drawn on the panel in pure white, but made indefinite by distance. The joyous swallows climb high into the illuminated air till the eye, daunted by the glow, can scarce detect their white breasts as they turn.

Slant shadows from the western side give but a margin of contrast; the rays are reflected through them, and they are only shadows of shadows. At the edges their faint sloping lines are seen in the air, where a million motes impart a fleeting solidity to the atmosphere. A pink-painted front, the golden eagle of the great West, golden lettering, every chance strip and speck of colour is washed in the dazzling light, made clear and evident. The hands and numerals of the clock yonder are distinct and legible, the white dial-plate polished; a window suddenly opened

[1] The sunlight and the winds enter London, and the life of the fields is there too, if you will but see it.

throws a flash across the square. Eastwards the air in front of the white walls quivers, heat and light reverberating visibly, and the dry flowers on the window sills burn red and yellow in the glare. Southwards green trees, far down the street, stand, as it seems, almost at the foot of the chiselled tower of Parliament—chiselled in straight lines and perpendicular grooves, each of which casts a shadow into itself. Again, the corners advanced before the main wall throw shadows on it, and the hollow casements draw shadows into their cavities. Thus, in the bright light against the blue sky the tower pencils itself with a dark crayon, and is built, not of stone, but of light and shadow. Flowing lines of water rise and fall from the fountains in the square, drooping like the boughs of a weeping ash, drifted a little to one side by an imperceptible air, and there sprinkling the warm pavement in a sparkling shower. The shower of finely divided spray now advances and now retreats, as the column of water bends to the current of air, or returns to its upright position.

By a pillared gateway there is a group in scarlet, and from time to time other groups in scarlet pass and repass within the barrack-court. A cream-tinted dress, a pink parasol—summer hues—go by in the stream of dark-clothed people; a flower fallen on the black water of a river. Either the light subdues the sound, or perhaps rather it renders the senses slumberous and less sensitive, but the great sunlit square is silent—silent, that is, for the largest city on earth. A slumberous silence of abundant light, of the full summer day, of the high flood of summer hours whose tide can rise no higher. A time to linger and dream under the beautiful breast of heaven, heaven brooding and descending in pure light upon man's handiwork. If the light shall thus come in, and of its mere loveliness overcome every aspect of dreariness, why shall not the light of thought, and hope—the light of the soul—overcome and sweep away the dust of our lives?

I stood under the portico of the National Gallery in the shade looking southwards, across the fountains and the lions, towards the green trees under the distant tower. Once a swallow sang in passing on the wing, garrulous still as in the time of old Rome and Augustan Virgil. From the high pediments dropped the occasional chatter of sparrows and the chirp of their young in the roofs. The second brood, they were late; they would not be in time for the harvest and the fields of stubble. A flight of blue pigeons rose from the central pavement to the level line of the parapet of the western houses. A starling shot across the square, swift, straight, resolute. I looked for the swifts, but they had gone, earliest of all to leave our sky for distant countries. Away in the harvest field the reaper, pausing in his work, had glanced up at the one stray fleck of cloud in the sky, which to my fancy might be a Cupid on a blue panel, and seeing it smiled in the midst of the corn, wiping his blackened face, for he knew it meant dry weather. Heat, and the dust of the straw, the violent labour had darkened his face from brown almost to blackness—a more than swarthiness, a blackness. The stray cloud was spreading out in filaments, each thread drawn to a fineness that ended presently in disappearance. It was a sign to him of continued sunshine and the prosperity of increased wages. The sun from whose fiery brilliance I escaped into the shadow was to him a welcome friend; his neck was bare to the fierceness of the sun. His heart was gladdened because the sky promised him permission to labour till the sinews of his fingers stiffened in their crooked shape (as they held the reaping hook), and he could hardly open them to grasp the loaf he had gained.

So men laboured of old time, whether with plough or

sickle or pruning-hook, in the days when Augustan Virgil
heard the garrulous swallow, still garrulous. An endless
succession of labour, under the brightness of summer,
under the gloom of winter; to my thought it is a sadness
even in the colour and light and glow of this hour of sun,
this ceaseless labour, repeating the furrow, reiterating the
blow, the same furrow, the same stroke—shall we never
know how to lighten it, how to live with the flowers, the
swallows, the sweet delicious shade, and the murmur of
the stream? Not the blackened reaper only, but the crowd
whose low hum renders the fountain inaudible, the nameless and unknown crowd of this immense city wreathed
round about the central square. I hope that at some time,
by dint of bolder thought and freer action, the world shall
see a race able to enjoy it without stint, a race able to
enjoy the flowers with which the physical world is strewn,
the colours of the garden of life. To look backwards with
the swallow there is sadness, to-day with the fleck of cloud
there is unrest; but forward, with the broad sunlight,
there is hope.

Except you see these colours, and light, and tones,
except you see the blue heaven over the parapet, you
know not, you cannot feel, how great are the possibilities
of man. At my back, within the gallery, there is many
a canvas painted under Italian skies, in glowing Spain, in
bright Southern France. There are scenes lit with the light
that gleams on orange grove and myrtle; there are faces
tinted with the golden hue that floats in southern air.
But yet, if any one impartial will stand here outside, under
the portico, and forgetting that it is prosaic London, will
look at the summer enclosed within the square, and
acknowledge it for itself as it is, he must admit that the
view—light and colour, tone and shade—is equal to the
painted canvas, is full, as it were, to the brim of interest,

suggestion, and delight. Before the painted canvas you stand with prepared mind; you have come to see Italy, you are educated to find colour, and the poetry of tone. Therefore you see it, if it is there. Here in the portico you are unprepared, uneducated; no one has ever given a thought of it. But now trace out the colour and the brightness; gaze up into the sky, watch the swallows, note the sparkle of the fountain, observe the distant tower chiselled with the light and shade. Think, then, of the people, not as mere buyers and sellers, as mere counters, but as human beings—beings possessed of hearts and minds, full of the passions and the hopes and fears which made the ancient poets great merely to record. These are the same passions that were felt in antique Rome, whose very name is a section of human life. There is colour in these lives now as then.

6

Nature near London

IT IS USUALLY SUPPOSED TO BE NECESSARY TO GO FAR into the country to find wild birds and animals in sufficient numbers to be pleasantly studied. Such was certainly my own impression till circumstances led me, for the convenience of access to London, to reside for a while about twelve miles from town. There my preconceived views on the subject were quite overthrown by the presence of as much bird-life as I had been accustomed to in distant fields and woods.

First, as the spring began, came crowds of chiff-chaffs and willow wrens filling the furze with ceaseless flutterings. Presently a nightingale sang in a hawthorn bush only just on the other side of the road. One morning, on looking out of the window, there was a hen pheasant in the furze almost underneath. Rabbits often came out into the spaces of grass between the bushes.

The furze itself became a broad surface of gold, beautiful to look down upon, with islands of tenderest birch green interspersed, and willows in which the sedge-reedling chattered. They used to say in the country that cuckoos were getting scarce, but here the notes of the cuckoo echoed all day long, and the birds often flew over the house. Doves cooed, blackbirds whistled, thrushes sang, jays called, wood-pigeons uttered the old familiar notes in the little copse hard by. Even a heron went over now and then, and in the evening from the window I could hear partridges calling each other to roost.

Along the roads and lanes the quantity and variety of

life in the hedges was really astonishing. Magpies, jays,
woodpeckers—both green and pied-kestrels hovering overhead, sparrow-hawks darting over gateways, hares by the
clover, weasels on the mounds, stoats at the edge of the
corn. I missed but two birds, the corncrake and the grass-
hopper lark, and found these another season. Two squirrels
one day ran along the palings and up into a guelder-rose
tree in the garden. As for the finches and sparrows their
number was past calculation. There was material for many
years' observation. . . .

The question may be asked: Why have you not in-
dicated in every case the precise locality where you were
so pleased? Why not mention the exact hedge, the particular meadow? Because no two persons look at the same
thing with the same eyes. To me this spot may be
attractive, to you another; a third thinks yonder gnarled
oak the most artistic. Nor could I guarantee that every
one should see the same things under the same conditions
of season, time or weather. How could I arrange for you
next autumn to see the sprays of the horse-chestnut,
scarlet from frost, reflected in the dark water of the brook?
There might not be any frost till all the leaves had dropped.
How could I contrive that the cuckoos should circle
round the copse, the sunlight glint upon the stream, the
warm sweet wind come breathing over the young corn
just when I should wish you to feel it? Every one must
find their own locality. I find a favourite wild-flower here,
and the spot is dear to me; you find yours yonder. Neither
painter nor writer can show the spectator their originals.
It would be very easy, too, to pass any of these places and
see nothing, or but little. Birds are wayward, wild creatures uncertain. The tree crowded with wood-pigeons one
minute is empty the next. To traverse the paths day by
day, and week by week; to keep an eye ever on the fields

from year's end to year's end, is the one only method of knowing what really is in, or comes to them. That the sitting gambler sweeps the board is true of these matters. The richest locality may be apparently devoid of interest just at the juncture of a chance visit.

Though my preconceived ideas were overthrown by the presence of so much that was beautiful and interesting close to London, yet in course of time I came to understand what was at first a dim sense of something wanting. In the shadiest lane, in the still pinewoods, on the hills of purple heath, after brief contemplation there arose a restlessness, a feeling that it was essential to be moving. In no grassy mead was there a nook where I could stretch myself in slumberous ease and watch the swallows ever wheeling, wheeling in the sky. This was the unseen influence of mighty London. The strong life of the vast city magnetized me, and I felt it under the calm oaks. The something wanting in the fields was the absolute quiet, peace, and rest which dwells in the meadows and under the trees and on the hilltops in the country. Under its power the mind gradually yields itself to the green earth, the wind among the trees, the song of birds, and comes to have an understanding with them all. For this it is still necessary to seek the far away glades and hollow combes, or to sit alone beside the sea.

7

A Wet Night in London

O PAQUE FROM RAIN DRAWN IN SLANT STREAKS BY wind and speed across the pane, the window of the railway carriage lets nothing be seen but stray flashes of red lights—the signals rapidly passed. Wrapped in thick overcoat, collar turned up to his ears, warm gloves on his hands, and a rug across his knees, the traveller may well wonder how those red signals and the points are worked out in the storms of wintry London. Rain blown in gusts through the misty atmosphere, gas and smoke-laden, deepens the darkness; the howl of the blast humming in the telegraph wires, hurtling round the chimney-pots on a level with the line, rushing up from the archways; steam from the engines, roar, and whistle, shrieking brakes, and grinding wheels—how is the traffic worked at night in safety over the inextricable windings of the iron roads into the City?

At London Bridge the door is opened by some one who gets out, and the cold air comes in; there is a rush of people in damp coats, with dripping umbrellas, and time enough to notice the archæologically interesting wooden beams which support the roof of the South-Eastern station. Antique beams they are, good old Norman oak, such as you may sometimes find in very old country churches that have not been restored, such as yet exist in Westminster Hall, temp. Rufus or Stephen, or so. Genuine old woodwork, worth your while to go and see. Take a sketch-book and make much of the ties and angles and bolts; ask Whistler or Macbeth, or some one to etch them, get the Royal Antiquarian Society to pay a visit and issue a pamphlet; gaze at them reverently and earnestly, for they are not easily to be matched in London. Iron girders and spacious roofs are the modern fashion; here we have the Middle Ages well-preserved—slam! the door is banged-to, onwards, over the invisible river, more red signals and rain, and finally the terminus. Five hundred well-dressed and civilized savages, wet, cross, weary, all anxious to get in—eager for home and dinner; five hundred stiffened and cramped folk equally eager to get out—mix on a narrow platform, with a train running off one side, and a detached engine gliding gently after it. Push, wriggle, wind in and out, bumps from portmanteaus, and so at last out into the street.

Now, how are you going to get into an omnibus? The street is "up", the traffic confined to half a narrow thoroughfare, the little space available at the side crowded with newsvendors whose contents bills are spotted and blotted with wet, crowded, too, with young girls, bonnet-less, with aprons over their heads, whose object is simply to do nothing—just to stand in the rain and chaff; the newsvendors yell their news in your ears, then, finding you don't purchase, they "Yah!" at you; an aged crone begs you to buy "lights"; a miserable young crone, with pinched face, offers artificial flowers—oh, Naples! Rush comes the rain, and the gas-lamps are dimmed; whoo-oo comes the wind like a smack; cold drops get in the ears and eyes; clean wristbands are splotched; greasy mud splashed over shining boots; some one knocks the umbrella round, and the blast all but turns it. "Wake up!"— "Now then—stop here all night?"—"Gone to sleep?" They shout, they curse, they put their hands to their mouths trumpet wise and bellow at each other, these cabbies, vanmen, 'busmen, all angry at the block in the

St Dunstan's Church
Fleet Street:
Sunday Evening

narrow way. The 'bus-driver, with London stout, and plenty of it, polishing his round cheeks like the brasswork of a locomotive, his neck well wound and buttressed with thick comforter and collar, heedeth not, but goes on his round, now fast, now slow, always stolid and rubicund, the rain running harmlessly from him as if he were oiled. The conductor, perched like the showman's monkey behind, hops and twists, and turns now on one foot and now on the other as if the plate were red-hot; now holds on with one hand, and now dexterously shifts his grasp; now shouts to the crowd and waves his hands towards the pavement, and again looks round the edge of the 'bus forwards and curses somebody vehemently. "Near side up! Look alive! Full inside"—curses, curses, curses; rain, rain, rain, and no one can tell which is most plentiful.

The cab-horse's head comes nearly inside the 'bus, the 'bus-pole threatens to poke the hansom in front; the brougham would be careful, for varnish sake, but is wedged and must take its chance; van-wheels catch omnibus hubs; hurry, scurry, whip, and drive; slip, slide, bump, rattle, jar, jostle, an endless stream clattering on, in, out, and round. On, on—"Stanley, on"—the first and last words of cabby's life; on, on, the one law of existence in a London street—drive on, stumble or stand, drive on—strain sinews, crack, splinter—drive on; what a sight to watch as you wait amid the newsvendors and bonnetless girls for the 'bus that will not come! Is it real? It seems like a dream, those nightmare dreams in which you know that you must run, and do run, and yet cannot lift the legs that are heavy as lead, with the demon behind pursuing, the demon of Drive-on. Move, or cease to be—pass out of Time or be stirring quickly; if you stand you must suffer even here on the pavement, splashed with greasy mud, shoved by coarse ruffianism, however good your intentions—just dare to stand still! Ideas here for moralizing, but I can't preach with the roar and the din and the wet in my ears, and the flickering street lamps flaring. That's the 'bus—no; the tarpaulin hangs down and obscures the inscription; yes. Hi! No heed; how could you be so confiding as to imagine conductor or driver would deign to see a signalling passenger; the game is to drive on.

A gentleman makes a desperate rush and grabs the handrail; his foot slips on the asphalt or wood, which is like oil, he slides, his hat totters; happily he recovers himself and gets in. In the block the 'bus is stayed a moment, and somehow we follow, and are landed—"somehow" advisedly. For how do we get into a 'bus? After the pavement, even this hard seat would be nearly an easy-chair, were it not for the damp smell of soaked overcoats, the ceaseless rumble, and the knockings overhead outside. The noise is immensely worse than the shaking or the steamy atmosphere, the noise ground into the ears, and wearying the mind to a state of drowsy narcotism—you become chloroformed through the sense of hearing, a condition of dreary resignation and uncomfortable ease. The illuminated shops seem to pass like an endless window without division of doors; there are groups of people staring in at them in spite of the rain; ill-clad, half-starving people for the most part; the well-dressed hurry onwards; they have homes. A dull feeling of satisfaction creeps over you that you are at least in shelter; the rumble is a little better than the wind and the rain and the puddles. If the Greek sculptors were to come to life again and cut us out in bas-relief for another Parthenon, they would have to represent us shuffling along, heads down and coat-tails flying, splash-splosh—a nation of umbrellas.

Under a broad archway, gaily lighted, the broad and happy way to a theatre, there is a small crowd waiting, and among them two ladies, with their backs to the photographs and bills, looking out into the street. They stand side by side, evidently quite oblivious and indifferent to the motley folk about them, chatting and laughing, taking the wet and windy wretchedness of the night as a joke. They are both plump and rosy-cheeked, dark eyes gleaming and red lips parted; both decidedly good-looking, much too rosy and full-faced, too well fed and comfortable to take a prize from Burne-Jones, very worldly people in the roast-beef sense. Their faces glow in the bright light—merry sea coal-fire faces; they have never turned their backs on the good things of this life. "Never shut the door on good fortune", as Queen Isabella of Spain says. Wind and rain may howl and splash, but here are two faces they never have touched—rags and battered shoes drift along the pavement—no wet feet or cold necks here. Best of all they glow with good spirits, they laugh, they chat; they are full of enjoyment, clothed thickly with health and happiness, as their shoulders—good wide shoulders—are thickly wrapped in warmest furs. The 'bus goes on, and they are lost to view; if you came back in an hour you would find them still there without doubt—still jolly, chatting, smiling, waiting perhaps for the stage, but anyhow far removed, like the goddesses on Olympus, from the splash and misery of London. Drive on.

The head of a great grey horse in a van drawn up by the pavement, the head and neck stand out and conquer the rain and misty dinginess by sheer force of beauty, sheer strength of character. He turns his head—his neck forms a fine curve, his face is full of intelligence, in spite of the half dim light and the driving rain, of the thick atmosphere, and the black hollow of the covered van behind, his head and neck stand out, just as in old portraits the face is still bright, though surrounded with crusted varnish. It would be a glory to any man to paint him. Drive on.

How strange the dim, uncertain faces of the crowd, half-seen, seem in the hurry and rain; faces held downwards and muffled by the darkness—not quite human in their eager and intensely concentrated haste. No one thinks of or notices another—on, on—splash, shove, and scramble; an intense selfishness, so selfish as not to be selfish, if that can be understood, so absorbed as to be past observing that any one lives but themselves. Human beings reduced to mere hurrying machines, worked by wind and rain, and stern necessities of life; driven on; something very hard and unhappy in the thought of this. They seem reduced to the condition of the wooden cabs— the mere vehicles—pulled along by the irresistible horse Circumstance. They shut their eyes mentally, wrap themselves in the overcoat of indifference, and drive on, drive on. It is time to get out at last. The 'bus stops on one side of the street, and you have to cross to the other. Look up and down—lights are rushing each way, but for the moment none are close. The gas-lamps shine in the puddles of thick greasy water, and by their gleam you can guide yourself round them. Cab coming! Surely he will give way a little and not force you into that great puddle; no, he neither sees, nor cares. Drive on, drive on. Quick! the shafts! Step in the puddle and save your life!

8

The Pigeons at
The British Museum

THE FRONT OF THE BRITISH MUSEUM STANDS IN THE sunlight clearly marked against the firm blue of the northern sky. The blue appears firm as if solid above the angle of the stonework, for while looking towards it—towards the north—the rays do not come through the azure, which is therefore colour without life. It seems nearer than the southern sky, it descends and forms a close background to the building; as you approach you seem to come nearer to the blue surface rising at its rear. The dark edges of sloping stone are distinct and separate, but not sharp; the hue of the stone is toned by time and weather, and is so indefinite as to have lost its hardness. Those small rounded bodies upon the cornice are pigeons resting in the sun, so motionless and neutral-tinted that they might be mistaken for some portion of the carving. A double gilt ring, a circle in a circle, at the feet of an allegorical figure gleams brightly against the dark surface. The sky already seems farther away seen between the boles of stone, perpetual shade dwells in their depth, but two or three of the pigeons fluttering down are searching for food on the sunlit gravel at the bottom of the steps. To them the building is merely a rock, pierced with convenient caverns; they use its exterior for their purpose, but penetrate no farther. With air and light, the sunlit gravel, the green lawn between it and the outer railings—with these they are concerned, and with these only. The heavy roll of the traffic in Oxford Street, audible here, is nothing to them; the struggle for money does not touch them, they let it go by. Nor the many minds searching and re-searching in the great Library, this mental toil is no more to them than the lading of the waggons in the street. Neither the tangible product nor the intellectual attainment is of any value—only the air and light. There are idols in the galleries within upon whose sculptured features the hot Eastern sun shone thousands of years since. They were made by human effort, however mistaken, and they were the outcome of human thought and handiwork. The doves fluttered about the temples in those days, full only of the air and light. They fluttered about the better temples of Greece and round the porticoes where philosophy was born. Still only the light, the sunlight, the air of heaven. We labour on and think, and carve our idols and the pen never ceases from its labour; but the lapse of the centuries has left us in the same place. The doves who have not laboured nor travailed in thought possess the sunlight. Is not theirs the preferable portion?

The shade deepens as I turn from the portico to the hall and vast domed house of books. The half-hearted light under the dome is stagnant and dead. For it is the nature of light to beat and throb; it has a pulse and undulation like the swing of the sea. Under the trees in the woodlands it vibrates and lives; on the hills there is a resonance of light. It beats against every leaf, and, thrown back, beats again; it is agitated with the motion of the grass blades; you can feel it ceaselessly streaming on your face. It is renewed and fresh every moment, and never twice do you see the same ray. Stayed and checked by the dome and book-built walls, the beams lose their elasticity, and the ripple ceases in the motionless pool. The eyes, responding, forget to turn quickly, and only partially see. Deeper thought and inspiration quit the heart, for they can only exist where the light vibrates and communicates its tone to the soul. If any imagine they shall find thought in many books, certainly they will be disappointed. Thought dwells by the stream and sea, by the hill and in the woodland, in the sunlight and free wind, where the wild dove haunts. Walls and roof shut it off as they shut off the undulation of light. The very lightning cannot penetrate here. A murkiness marks the coming of the cloud, and the dome becomes vague, but the fierce flash is shorn to a pale reflection, and the thunder is no more than the rolling of a heavier truck loaded with tomes. But in closing out the sky, with it is cut off all that the sky can tell you with its light, or in its passion of storm.

Sitting at these long desks and trying to read, I soon find that I have made a mistake; it is not here I shall find that which I seek. Yet the magic of books draws me here time after time, to be as often disappointed. Something in a book tempts the mind as pictures tempt the eye; the eye grows weary of pictures, but looks again. The mind wearies of books, yet cannot forget that once when they were first opened in youth they gave it hope of knowledge. Those first books exhausted, there is nothing left but words and covers. It seems as if all the books in the world—really books—can be bought for £10. Man's whole thought is purchasable at that small price, for the value of a watch, of a good dog. For the rest it is repetition and paraphrase. The grains of wheat were threshed out and garnered two thousand years since. Except the receipts of chemists, except specifications for the steam-engine, or the electric motor, there is nothing in these millions of books that was not known at the commencement of our era. Not a thought has been added. Continual threshing has widened out the heap of straw and spread it abroad, but it is empty. Nothing will ever be found in it. Those original grains of true thought were found beside the stream, the sea, in the sunlight, at the shady verge of woods. Let us leave this beating and turning-over of empty straw; let us return to the stream and the hills; let us ponder by night in view of the stars.

It is pleasant to go out again into the portico under the great columns. On the threshold I feel nearer knowledge than when within. The sun shines, and southwards above the houses there is a statue crowning the summit of some building. The figure is in the midst of the light; it stands out clear and white as if in Italy. The southern blue is luminous—the beams of light flow through it—the air is full of the undulation and life of light. There is rest in gazing at the sky: a sense that wisdom does exist and may be found, a hope returns that was taken away among the books. The green lawn is pleasant to look at, though it is mown so ruthlessly. If they would only let the grass spring up, there would be a thought somewhere entangled in the long blades as a dewdrop sparkles in their depths. Seats should be placed here, under the great columns or by the grass, so that one might enjoy the sunshine after books and watch the pigeons.[1] They have no fear of the people, they come to my feet, but the noise of a door heavily swinging-to in the great building alarms them; they rise and float round, and return again. The sunlight casts a shadow of the pigeon's head and neck upon his shoulder; he turns his head, and the shadow of his beak falls on his breast. Iridescent gleams of bronze and green and blue play about his neck; blue predominates. His pink feet step so near, the red round his eye is visible. As he rises vertically, forcing his way in a straight line upwards, his wings almost

[1] See Note 8.

The British Museum

meet above his back and again beneath the body; they are put forth to his full stroke. When his flight inclines and becomes gradually horizontal, the effort is less and the wing tips do not approach so closely.

They have not laboured in mental searching as we have; they have not wasted their time looking among empty straw for the grain that is not there. They have been in the sunlight. Since the days of ancient Greece the doves have remained in the sunshine; we who have laboured have found nothing. In the sunshine, by the shady verge of woods, by the sweet waters where the wild dove sips, there alone will thought be found.

9

Fleet Street

Portrait of a Bohemian

I

IF I COULD BUT WRITE THE INSIDE HISTORY OF FLEET Street, I should be looked upon as the most wonderful exponent of human life that had ever touched a pen. Balzac—whom everybody talks of and nobody has read, because the discrimination of Paternoster Row has refused him a translation till quite lately—Zola, who professes to be realistic, who is nothing if not realistic, but whose writings are so curiously crude and merely skim the surface; even the great Hugo, who produced the masterpiece of all fiction, "Les Misérables"; all three of them, the entire host of manuscript makers, I am sure I could vanquish them all, if I could only write the inside life of Fleet Street.

Not in any grace of style or sweeping march of diction, but just pencil-jotted in the roughest words to hand, just as rich and poor, well-dressed ladies and next-door beggars are bundled into a train, so, without choice of language, but hustling the first words anyhow, as it were, into the first compartment. If I could only get Alere to tell me all he had seen in Fleet Street, and could just jot it down on the margin of a stained newspaper, all the world would laugh and weep. For such things do go on in Fleet Street as no man has written yet.

If only Victor Hugo were alive and young again!

Alere liked pulling off the proofs in his shirt-sleeves,

swigging his stout, smoking on the sly (smoking was forbidden in his workshop), working with all the genius of an inspired mechanic one moment and dropping into absolute idleness the next, spending infinite pains in finishing one bit of work, as if his very life depended on the smoothing of an edge of paper, putting off the next till the end of the month, pottering, sleeping, gossiping, dreaming over old German works, and especially dreaming over Goethe, humming old songs—for he had been a great traveller—sometimes scrawling a furious Mazzinian onslaught in a semi-Nihilist foreign print, collecting stray engravings, wandering hither and thither.

Alere Flamma, artist, engraver, bookbinder, connoisseur, traveller, printer, Republican, conspirator, sot, smoker, dreamer, poet, kind-hearted, good-natured, prodigal, shiftless, man of Fleet Street, carpet-bag man, gentleman shaken to pieces . . .

In London he never wore a collar, only a bright red scarf round his neck; the company he kept would have shunned him—they would have looked him up and down disdainfully: "Got a collar on—had no breakfast." They would have scornfully regarded him as no better than a City clerk, the class above all others scorned by those who use tools.

"Got a collar on—had no breakfast." The City clerk, playing the Masher on thirty shillings a week, goes without food to appear the gentleman.

Alere, the artist, drank with the men who used hammer, and file, or set up type—a godless set, these setters up of type at four o'clock in the morning; oysters and stout at 4 a.m., special taverns they must have open for them—open before the sun gleams in the East—Oh! Fleet, Fleet Street, what a place it is!

By no possible means could Alere work himself into

E

a dress coat. Could he have followed the celebrated advice—"You put on a dress coat and go into society"—he would soon have become a name, a fame, a taker of big fees, a maker of ten thousand yearly.

To a man who could draw like Alere, possessed, too, of the still rarer talent—the taste to see what to draw—there really is no limit in our days; for as for colour, you do not require a genius for colour in an age of dinginess—why, the point, nowadays, is to avoid colour, and in a whole Academy you shall scarcely find as much as would tint a stick of sealing-wax.

"You put on a black coat and go into society"—that is the secret of commissions, and commissions are fortune. Nothing so clever in the way of advice has been sent forth as that remark. The great Tichborne claimant said something about folk that had money and no brains, and folk that had brains but no money; and "they as has no brains ought to be so managed as to supply money to those who had." But even the greatness of the great Tichborne's observation falls into insignificance before Chesterfield in one sentence: "Put on a black coat and go into society."

What are the sayings of the seven wise men of Greece compared to *that*?

By no possible means could Alere Flamma work himself into a dress coat. The clubs, the houses of the great, the mutual admiration dinners—those great institutions of the day—were all closed to him because of the Dress Coat.

If he had really desired to enter, of course he would have squeezed into the evening monkey-skin somehow; but, in truth, Alere did not want to enter.

Inside he might have finished a portrait a month. . . . What he actually did was to make designs for book-covers—magnificent book-covers that will one day fetch their weight in bank-notes—manipulating a good deal of

it himself—"tooling"—for the libraries of noble con-
noisseurs. . . .

For a week's work—say half-an-hour a day—he got
perhaps about ten pounds. With the ten pounds he was
satisfied—ten pounds represents a good deal of brandy, or
stout, or even wine, about as much as one man can manage
at a bout; besides tobacco, the gallery at the theatre, and
innumerable trifles of that kind. Ten pounds represents a
good deal of street life.

Sometimes he drew—and engraved—illustrations for
books, being as clever with the engraver's tools as with
the pencil; sometimes he cut out those odd, fantastic
"initials", "ornaments", "finials", which are now so
commonly seen in publications, catching the classical
grotesque of the Renaissance to perfection, and deceiving
the experienced; sometimes he worked in the press-room
in the House of Flamma, Fleet Street, pulling artists'
proofs, or printing expensively illustrated volumes—
numbered, and the plates destroyed—actual manual work,
in his shirt sleeves.

He could stop when he liked and take a swig of stout.
That was the Alere style.

Smoking was forbidden in the old House of Flamma
because of the worm-eaten beams, the worm-eaten rafters
and staircase, the dusty, decayed bookshelves, the dry,
rotten planks of the floor, the thin wooden partitions, all
ready to catch fire at the mere sight of a match. Also
because of the piles of mouldy books which choked the
place, and looked fit for nothing but a bonfire, but which
were worth thousands of pounds; the plates and lithographic stones, artists' proofs, divers and sundry Old
Masters in a room upstairs, all easily destructible.

But Alere, being a son of the house, though not in
command, did not choose to be amenable to rules and

orders in fact, in fiction he was. He smoked and kept the glue-pot ready on the stove; if a certain step was known to be approaching the pipe was thrust out of sight, and some dry glue set melting, the powerful incense quite hiding the flavour of tobacco. A good deal of dry glue is used in London in this way. . . .

II

In his rooms at his lodgings there were literally hundreds of sketches, done on all sorts and sizes of paper, from the inside of an envelope hastily torn open to elephant. The bureau was full of them, crammed in anyhow, neither sorted nor arranged; nothing, of course, could be found when it was wanted. The drawers of the bookcase—it was his own furniture—were full of them; the writing-table drawer; a box in one corner; some were on the mantelpiece smoked and gritty; some inside his books most of which were interleaved in this manner; literally hundreds of sketches, the subjects as numerous and varied.

Views in English country lanes, views on the Danube, bands playing in band-loving Vienna, old Highgate Arch-way, studies from Canterbury Cathedral, statuary in the Louvre, ships battling with the wind in the North Sea— a savage fight between sail and gale—horses in the meadow, an aged butler, a boy whipping a top, charcoal burners in the Black Forest, studies from the nude— Parisian models, Jewesses, almost life-size, a drayman heaving up a huge tankard, overshadowing his face like Mount Atlas turned over his thumb, designs to illustrate classical mythology, outlines expressing the ideas of Goethe—outlines of Marguerite and Faust among the roses—"He loves me; he loves me not," big-armed Flemish beauties with breasts as broad as the Zuyder-Zee was deep in the song, roofs of Nuremburg, revolutionary heroes charging their muskets in the famous year '48, when Alere had a bullet through his hat, in Vienna, I think; no end to them.

Sometimes when Alere had done no work for a month or two, and his ten pounds were spent, if he wanted a few guineas he would take a small selection of these round to the office of a certain illustrated paper; the Editor would choose, and hand over the money at once, well aware that it was ready money his friend needed. They were not exactly friends—there are no friends in London, only acquaintances—but a little chummy, because the Editor himself had had a fiery youth, and they had met in sunny Wien. That was the only paper that ever got sketches out of Alere.

If only Alere would have gone and sketched what he was *asked* to sketch! Ah! there is the difference; he could not do it, his nature would not let him; he could draw what he saw with his own eyes, but not what other people wanted him to see. A merry income he might have made if he would only have consented to see what other eyes— common, vulgar eyes—wanted to see, and which he could so easily have drawn for them.

Out of these piles of varied sketches there were two kinds the Editor instantly snapped at: the one was wild flowers, the other little landscape bits.

Wild flowers were his passion. They were to Flamma as Juliet to Romeo. Romeo's love, indeed, rushed up like straw on fire, a great blaze of flame; he perished in it as the straw; perhaps he might not have worshipped Juliet next year. Flamma had loved his wild flowers close upon forty years, ever since he could remember; most likely longer, for doubtless the dumb infant loved the daisies put in his chubby hand.

His passion they were still as he drew near fifty, and saw all things become commonplace. That is the saddest of thoughts—as we grow older the romance fades, and all things become commonplace.

Half our lives are spent in wishing for to-morrow, the other half in wishing for yesterday.

Wild flowers alone never become commonplace. The white wood-sorrel at the foot of the oak, the violet in the hedge of the vale, the thyme on the wind-swept downs, they were as fresh this year as last, as dear to-day as twenty years since, even dearer, for they grow now, as it were, in the earth we have made for them of our hopes, our prayers, our emotions, our thoughts.

Sketch-book upon sketch-book in Alere's room was full of wild flowers, drawn as he had found them in the lanes and woods at Coombe Oaks—by the footpaths, by the lake and the lesser ponds, on the hills—as he had found them, not formed into an artificial design, not torn up by the roots, or cut and posed for the occasion— exactly as they were when his eye caught sight of them. A difficult thing to do, but Alere did it. . . .

These flowers the Editor bought eagerly, and the little landscapes. From a stile, beside a rick, through a gap in the hedge, odd, unexpected places, Alere caught a view of the lake, the vale, the wood, groups of trees, old houses, and got them in his magical way on a few square inches of paper. They were very valuable for book illustration. They were absolutely true to nature and fact. . . .

III

When a man once gets into Fleet Street he cannot get out.

Conventionally, I suppose, it would be the right thing

to represent Alere as a great genius neglected, or as a genius destroyed by intemperance. The conventional type is so easy—so accepted—so popular; it would pay better, perhaps, to make him out a victim in some way.

He was not neglected, neither was he the victim of intemperance in the usual sense.

The way to fame and fortune had always been wide open to him; there were long intervals when he did not drink, nor did drink enfeeble his touch; it was not half so much to struggle against as the chest diseases from which professional men so often suffer; I believe if he had really tried or wished he could have conquered his vice altogether. Neither of these causes kept him from the foremost rank.

There was no ambition, and there was no business-avarice. So many who have no ideal are kept hard at work by the sheer desire of money, and thus spurred onward, achieve something approaching greatness. Alere did not care for money.

He could not get out of Fleet Street. . . .

Something in Fleet Street holds tight those who once come within its influence. The cerebellum of the world, the "grey matter" of the world's brain, lies somewhere thereabouts. The thoughts of our time issue thence, like the radiating spokes of a wheel, to all places of the earth. There you have touch of the throbbing pulse of the vast multitudes that live and breathe. Their ideas come from Fleet Street.

From the printing-press and the engraver's wood-block, the lithographic-stone, the etcher's plate, from book and magazine, periodical and pamphlet, from world-read news-paper.

From Fleet Street, the centre whence ideas flow, outwards.

It is joyous to be in the flower-grown meads; it is sweet to be on the hill-top; delicious to feel the swell and the long roll of the hexameter of the seas; doubtless there is a wild rapture on the summit of the Himalayas; triumph in the heart of the African explorer at the river's source. But if once the mind has been dipped in Fleet Street, let the meads be never so sweet, the mountain-top never so exalted, still to Fleet Street the mind will return, because there is that other Mind, without whose sympathy even success is nothing—the Mind of the world.

I am, of course, thinking not only of the thoroughfare, Fleet Street, but of all that the printing-press means.

Alere was no leader of thought, but it was necessary to him to live and breathe in the atmosphere of thought— to feel the throb and swell around him—to be near the "grey matter" of the world's brain.

Once a man gets into Fleet Street he cannot get out . . . The flame must be fed.

Sad things happen on the stones of Fleet Street; if I could but get at it all to write the inside life of it, it would, indeed, be a book. Stone-cold poverty hovers about. The rich, living in the fool's paradise of money, think they know life, but they do not, for, as was said of the sea,

> *Only those who share its dangers*
> *Comprehend its mystery.*

Only those who have shared the struggle literally for bread—for a real, actual loaf—understand the dread realities of man's existence.

The HALL:
Charterhouse

10

Trees about Town

JUST OUTSIDE LONDON THERE IS A CIRCLE OF FINE, large houses, each standing in its own grounds, highly rented, and furnished with every convenience money can supply. If any one will look at the trees and shrubs growing in the grounds about such a house, chosen at random for an example, and make a list of them, he may then go round the entire circumference of Greater London, mile after mile, many days' journey, and find the list ceaselessly repeated.

There are acacias, sumachs, cedar deodaras, araucarias, laurels, planes, beds of rhododendrons, and so on. There are various other foreign shrubs and trees whose names have not become familiar, and then the next grounds contain exactly the same, somewhat differently arranged. Had they all been planted by Act of Parliament, the result could scarcely have been more uniform.

If, again, search were made in these enclosures for English trees and English shrubs, it would be found that none have been introduced. The English trees, timber trees, that are there, grew before the house was built; for the rest, the products of English woods and hedge-rows have been carefully excluded. The law is, "Plant planes, laurels, and rhododendrons; root up everything natural to this country."

To those who have any affection for our own wood-lands this is a pitiful spectacle, produced, too, by the expenditure of large sums of money. Will no one break through the practice, and try the effect of English trees? There is no lack of them, and they far excel anything yet imported in beauty and grandeur.

Though such suburban grounds mimic the isolation and retirement of ancient country houses surrounded with parks, the distinctive feature of the ancient houses is omitted. There are no massed bodies, as it were, of our own trees to give a substance to the view. Are young oaks ever seen in those grounds so often described as park-like? Some time since it was customary for the builder carefully to cut down every piece of timber on the property before putting in the foundations.

Fortunately, the influence of a better taste now pre-serves such trees as chance to be growing on the site at the moment it is purchased. These remain, but no others are planted. A young oak is not to be seen. The oaks that are there drop their acorns in vain, for if one takes root it is at once cut off; it would spoil the laurels. It is the same with elms; the old elms are decaying, and no successors are provided.

As for ash, it is doubtful if a young ash is anywhere to be found; if so, it is an accident. The ash is even rarer than the rest. In their places are put more laurels, cedar deodaras, various evergreens, rhododendrons, planes. How tame and insignificant are these compared with the oak! Thrice a year the oaks become beautiful in a different way.

In spring the opening buds give the tree a ruddy hue; in summer the great head of green is not to be surpassed; in autumn, with the falling leaf and acorn, they appear buff and brown. The nobility of the oak casts the pitiful laurel into utter insignificance. With elms it is the same; they are reddish with flower and bud very early in the year, the fresh leaf is a tender green; in autumn they are sometimes one mass of yellow.

Ashes change from almost black to a light green, then a deeper green, and again light green and yellow. Where is the foreign evergreen in the competition? Put side by side, competition is out of the question; you have only to get an artist to paint the oak in its three phases to see this. There is less to be said against the deodara than the rest, as it is a graceful tree; but it is not English in any sense.

The point, however, is that the foreigners oust the English altogether. Let the cedar and the laurel, and the whole host of invading evergreens, be put aside by themselves, in a separate and detached shrubbery, maintained for the purpose of exhibiting strange growths. Let them not crowd the lovely English trees out of the place. Planes are much planted now, with ill effect; the blotches where the bark peels, the leaves which lie on the sward like brown leather, the branches wide apart and giving no shelter to birds—in short, the whole ensemble of the plane is unfit for our country.

It was selected for London plantations, as the Thames Embankment, because its peeling bark was believed to protect it against the deposit of sooty particles, and because it grows quickly. For use in London itself it may be preferable; for semi-country seats, as the modern houses surrounded with their own grounds assume to be, it is unsightly. It has no association. No one has seen a plane in a hedgerow, or a wood, or a copse. There are no fragments of English history clinging to it as there are to the oak.

If trees of the plane class be desirable, sycamores may be planted, as they have in a measure become acclimatized. If trees that grow fast are required, there are limes and horse-chestnuts; the lime will run a race with any tree. The lime, too, has a pale yellow blossom, to which bees resort in numbers, making a pleasant hum, which seems the natural accompaniment of summer sunshine. Its leaves are put forth early.

Horse-chestnuts, too, grow quickly and without any attention, the bloom is familiar, and acknowledged to be fine, and in autumn the large sprays of leaves take orange and even scarlet tints. The plane is not to be mentioned beside either of them. Other trees as well as the plane would have flourished on the Thames Embankment, in consequence of the current of fresh air caused by the river. Imagine the Embankment with double rows of oaks, elms, or beeches; or, if not, even with limes or horse-chestnuts! To these certainly birds would have resorted— possibly rooks, which do not fear cities. On such a site the experiment would have been worth making.

If in the semi-country seats fast-growing trees are needed, there are, as I have observed, the lime and horse-chestnut; and if more variety be desired, add the Spanish chestnut and the walnut. The Spanish chestnut is a very fine tree; the walnut, it is true, grows slowly. If as many beeches as cedar deodaras and laurels and planes were planted in these grounds, in due course of time the tap of the woodpecker would be heard: a sound truly worth ten thousand laurels. At Kew, far closer to town than many of the semi-country seats are now, all our trees flourish in perfection.

Hardy birches, too, will grow in thin soil. Just compare the delicate drooping boughs of birch—they could not have been more delicate if sketched with a pencil—compare these with the gaunt planes!

Of all the foreign shrubs that have been brought to these shores, there is not one that presents us with so beautiful a spectacle as the bloom of the common old English hawthorn in May. The mass of blossom, the

pleasant fragrance, its divided and elegant leaf, place it
far above any of the importations. Besides which, the
traditions and associations of the May give it a human
interest.

The hawthorn is a part of natural English life—country
life. It stands side by side with the Englishman, as the
palm tree is pictured side by side with the Arab. You
cannot pick up an old play, or book of the time when old
English life was in the prime, without finding some
reference to the hawthorn. There is nothing of this in
the laurel, or any shrub whatever that may be thrust in
with a ticket to tell you its name; it has a ticket because
it has no interest, or else you would know it.

For use there is nothing like hawthorn; it will trim into
a thick hedge, defending the enclosure from trespassers,
and warding off the bitter winds; or it will grow into
a tree. Again, the old hedge-crab—the common, despised
crab-apple—in spring is covered with blossom, such
a mass of blossom that it may be distinguished a mile. Did
any one ever see a plane or a laurel look like that?

How pleasant, too, to see the clear white flower of the
blackthorn come out in the midst of the bitter easterly
breezes! It is like a white handkerchief beckoning to the
sun to come. There will not be much more frost; if the
wind is bitter to-day, the sun is rapidly gaining power.
Probably, if a blackthorn bush were by any chance discovered in the semi-parks or enclosures alluded to, it
would at once be rooted out as an accursed thing. The
very brambles are superior; there is the flower, the sweet
berry, and afterwards the crimson leaves—three things in
succession.

What can the world produce equal to the June rose?
The common briar, the commonest of all, offers a flower
which, whether in itself, or the moment of its appearance

at the juncture of all sweet summer things, or its history and associations, is not to be approached by anything a millionaire could purchase. The labourer casually gathers it as he goes to his work in the field, and yet none of the rich families whose names are synonymous with wealth can get anything to equal it if they ransack the earth.

After these, fill every nook and corner with hazel, and make filbert walks. Up and down such walks men strolled with rapiers by their sides while our admirals were hammering at the Spaniards with culverin and demi-cannon, and looked at the sun-dial and adjourned for a game at bowls, wishing that they only had a chance to bowl shot instead of peaceful wood. Fill in the corners with nut-trees, then, and make filbert walks. All these are like old story books, and the old stories are always best.

Still, there are others for variety, as the wild guelder rose, which produces heavy bunches of red berries; dogwood, whose leaves when frost-touched take deep colours; barberry, yielding a pleasantly acid fruit; the wayfaring tree; not even forgetting the elder, but putting it at the outside, because, though flowering, the scent is heavy, and because the elder was believed of old time to possess some of the virtue now attributed to the blue gum, and to neutralize malaria by its own odour.

For colour add the wild broom and some furze. Those who have seen broom in full flower, golden to the tip of every slender bough, cannot need any persuasion, surely, to introduce it. Furze is specked with yellow when the skies are dark and the storms sweep around, besides its prime display. Let wild clematis climb wherever it will. Then laurels may come after these, put somewhere by themselves, with their thick changeless leaves, unpleasant to the touch; no one ever gathers a spray.

Rhododendrons it is unkind to attack, for in themselves

they afford a rich flower. It is not the rhododendron, but the abuse of it, which must be protested against. Whether the soil suits or not—and, for the most part, it does not suit—rhododendrons are thrust in everywhere. Just walk in amongst them—behind the show—and look at the spindly, crooked stems, straggling how they may, and then look at the earth under them, where not a weed even will grow. The rhododendron is admirable in its place, but it is often overdone and a failure, and has no right to exclude those shrubs that are fitter. Most of the foreign shrubs about these semi-country seats look exactly like the stiff and painted little wooden trees that are sold for children's toys, and, like the toys, are the same colour all the year round.

Now, if you enter a copse in spring the eye is delighted with cowslips on the banks where the sunlight comes, with blue-bells, or earlier with anemones and violets, while later the ferns rise. But enter the semi-parks of the semi-country seat, with its affected assumption of country-ness, and there is not one of these. The fern is actually purposely eradicated—just think! Purposely! Though indeed they would not grow, one would think, under rhododendrons and laurels, cold-blooded laurels. They will grow under hawthorn, ash, or beside the bramble bushes.

If there chance to be a little pond or "fountain", there is no such thing as a reed, or a flag, or a rush. How the rushes would be hastily hauled out and hurled away with execrations!

Besides the greater beauty of English trees, shrubs, and plants, they also attract the birds, without which the grandest plantation is a vacancy, and another interest, too, arises from watching the progress of their growth and the advance of the season. Our own trees and shrubs literally keep pace with the stars which shine in our northern skies.

An astronomical floral almanack might almost be constructed, showing how, as the constellations marched on by night, the buds and leaves and flowers appeared by day.

The lower that brilliant Sirius sinks in the western sky after ruling the winter heavens, and the higher that red Arcturus rises, so the buds thicken, open, and bloom. When the Pleiades begin to rise in the early evening, the leaves are turning colour, and the seed vessels of the flowers take the place of the petals. The coincidences of floral and bird life, and of these with the movements of the heavens, impart a sense of breadth to their observation.

It is not only the violet or the anemone, there are the birds coming from immense distances to enjoy the summer with us; there are the stars appearing in succession, so that the most distant of objects seems brought into connection with the nearest, and the world is made one. The sharp distinction, the line artificially drawn between things, quite disappears when they are thus associated.

Birds, as just remarked, are attracted by our own trees and shrubs. Oaks are favourites with rooks and wood-pigeons; blackbirds whistle in them in spring; if there is a pheasant about in autumn he is sure to come under the oak; jays visit them. Elms are resorted to by most of the larger birds. Ash plantations attract wood-pigeons and turtle-doves. Thrushes are fond of the ash, and sing much on its boughs. The beech is the woodpecker's tree so soon as it grows old—birch one of the missel-thrush's.

In blackthorn the long-tailed tit builds the domed nest every one admires. Under the cover of brambles white-throats build. Nightingales love hawthorn, and so does every bird. Plant the hawthorn, and almost every bird will come to it, from the wood-pigeon down to the wren. Do not clear away the fallen branches and brown leaves, sweeping the plantation as if it were the floor of a ballroom, for it is just the tangle and the wilderness that brings the birds, and they like the disarray.

If evergreens are wanted, there are the yew, the box, and holly—all three well sanctioned by old custom. Thrushes will come for the y⁀ berries, and birds are fond of building in the thick cover of high box hedges. Notwithstanding the prickly leaves, they slip in and out of the holly easily. A few bunches of rushes and sedges, with some weeds and aquatic grasses, allowed to grow about a pond, will presently bring moorhens. Bare stones—perhaps concrete—will bring nothing.

If a bough falls into the water, let it stay; sparrows will perch on it to drink. If a sandy drinking-place can be made for them the number of birds that will come in the course of the day will be surprising.

Kind-hearted people, when winter is approaching, should have two posts sunk in their grounds, with planks across at the top; a raised platform with the edges projecting beyond the posts, so that cats cannot climb up, and of course higher than a cat can spring. The crumbs cast out upon this platform would gather crowds of birds; they will come to feel at home, and in spring time will return to build and sing.

F

Flocks of Birds about London

A CERTAIN ROAD LEADING OUTWARDS FROM A SUBURB, enters at once among fields. It soon passes a thick hedge dividing a meadow from a cornfield, in which hedge is a spot where some bluebells may be found in spring. Wild flowers are best seen when in masses, a few scattered along a bank much concealed by grass and foliage are lost, except indeed, upon those who love them for their own sake.

This meadow in June, for instance, when the butter-cups are high, is one broad expanse of burnished gold. The most careless passer-by can hardly fail to cast a glance over acres of rich yellow. The furze, again, especially after a shower has refreshed its tint, must be seen by all. Where broom grows thickly, lifting its colour well into view, or where the bird's-foot lotus in full summer overruns the thin grass of some upland pasture, the eye cannot choose but acknowledge it. So, too, with charlock, and with hill sides purple with heath, or where the woodlands are azure with bluebells for a hundred yards together. Learning from this, those who would transplant wild flowers to their garden should arrange to have as many as possible of the same species close together.

The bluebells in this hedge are unseen, except by the rabbits. The latter have a large burrow, and until the grass is too tall, or after it is cut or grazed, can be watched from the highway. In this hedge the first nightingale of the year sings, beginning some two or three days before the bird which comes to the bushes in the gorse, which will presently be mentioned.

It is, or rather was, a favourite meadow with the partridges; one summer there was, I think, a nest in or near it, for I saw the birds there daily. But the next year they were absent. One afternoon a brace of partridges came over the hedge within a few inches of my head; they had been flushed and frightened at some distance, and came with the wind at a tremendous pace. It is a habit with partridges to fly low, but just skimming the tops of the hedges, and certainly, had they been three inches lower, they must have taken my hat off. The knowledge that partridges were often about there made me always glance into this field on passing it, long after the nesting season was over.

In October, as I looked as usual, a hawk flew between the elms, and out into the centre of the meadow, with a large object in his talons. He alighted in the middle, so as to be as far as possible from either hedge, and no doubt prepared to enjoy his quarry, when something startled him, and he rose again. Then, as I got a better view, I saw it was a rat he was carrying. The long body of the animal was distinctly visible, and the tail depending, the hawk had it by the shoulders or head. Flying without the least apparent effort, the bird cleared the elms, and I lost sight of him beyond them. Now, the kestrel is but a small bird, and taking into consideration the size of the bird, and the weight of a rat, it seems as great a feat in proportion as for an eagle to snatch up a lamb.

Some distance up the road, and in the corner of an arable field, there was a wheat rick which was threshed and most of the straw carted away. But there still remained the litter, and among it probably a quantity of stray corn. There was always a flock of sparrows on this litter— a flock that might often be counted by the hundred. As I came near the spot one day a sparrowhawk, whose approach I had not observed, and which had therefore been flying low, suddenly came over the hedge just by the loose straw.

With shrill cries the sparrows instantly rushed for the hedge, not two yards distant; but the hawk, dashing through the crowd of them as they rose, carried away a victim. It was done in the tenth of a second. He came, singled his bird, and was gone like the wind, before the whirr of wings had ceased on the hawthorn where the flock cowered.

Another time, but in a different direction, I saw a hawk descend and either enter, or appear to enter, a short much-cropped hedge, but twenty yards distant. I ran to the spot; the hawk of course made off, but there was nothing in the bush save a hedge sparrow, which had probably attracted him, but which he had not succeeded in getting.

Kestrels are almost common; I have constantly seen them while strolling along the road, generally two together, and once three. In the latter part of the summer and autumn they seem to be most numerous, hovering over the recently reaped fields. Certainly there is no scarcity of hawks here. Upon one occasion, on Surbiton Hill, I saw a large bird of the same kind, but not sufficiently near to identify. From the gliding flight, the long forked tail, and large size I supposed it to be a kite. The same bird was going about next day, but still farther off. I cannot say that it was a kite, for unless it is a usual haunt, it is not in my opinion wise to identify positively a bird seen for so short a time.

The thick hedge mentioned is a favourite resort of blackbirds, and on a warm May morning, after a shower —they are extremely fond of a shower—half a dozen may be heard at once whistling in the elms. They use the elms here because there are not many oaks; the oak is the blackbird's favourite song-tree. There was one one day whistling with all his might on the lower branch of an elm, at the very roadside, and just above him a wood-pigeon was perched. A pair of turtle-doves built in the same hedge one spring, and while resting on the gate by the roadside their "coo-coo" mingled with the song of the nightingale and thrush, the blackbird's whistle, the chiff-chaff's "chip-chip", the willow-wren's pleading voice, and the rustle of green corn as the wind came rushing (as it always does to a gateway).

Goldfinches come by occasionally, not often, but still they do come. The rarest bird seems to be the bullfinch. I have only seen bullfinches three or four times in three seasons, and then only a pair. Now, this is worthy of note, as illustrating what I have often ventured to say about the habitat of birds being so often local, for if judged by observation here the bullfinch would be said to be a scarce bird by London. But it has been stated upon the best authority that only a few miles distant, and still nearer town, they are common.

The road now becomes bordered by elms on either side, forming an irregular avenue. Almost every elm in spring has its chaffinch loudly challenging. The birdcatchers are aware that it is a frequented resort, and on Sunday mornings four or five of them used to be seen in the course of a mile, each with a call bird in a partly darkened cage, a stuffed dummy, and limed twigs. In the corn fields on either hand wood-pigeons are numerous in spring and autumn. Up to April they come in flocks, feeding on the newly-sown grain when they can get at it, and varying it with ivy berries, from the ivy growing up the elms. By degrees the flocks break up as the nesting begins in earnest.

Some pair and build much earlier than others; in fact, the first egg recorded is very little to be depended on as an indication. Particular pairs (of many kinds of birds) may have nests, and yet the species as a species may be still flying in large packs. The flocks which settle in these fields number from one to two hundred. Rooks, wood-pigeons, and tame white pigeons often feed amicably mixed up together; the white tame birds are conspicuous at a long distance before the crops have risen, or after the stubble is ploughed.

I should think that the corn farmers of Surrey lose more grain from the birds than the agriculturists whose tenancies are a hundred miles from London. In the comparatively wild or open districts to which I had been accustomed before I made these observations I cannot recollect ever seeing such vast numbers of birds. There were places, of course, where they were numerous, and there were several kinds more represented than is the case here, and some that are scarcely represented at all. I have seen flocks of wood-pigeons immensely larger than any here; but then it was only occasionally. They came, passed over, and were gone. Here the flocks, though not very numerous, seem always to be about.

Sparrows crowd every hedge and field, their numbers are incredible; chaffinches are not to be counted; of green-finches there must be thousands. From the railway even you can see them. I caught glimpses of a ploughed field recently sown one spring from the window of a railway carriage, every little clod of which seemed alive with small birds, principally sparrows, chaffinches, and greenfinches. There must have been thousands in that field alone. In autumn the numbers are even greater, or rather more apparent. . . .

The first spring I resided in Surrey I was fairly astonished and delighted at the bird life which proclaimed itself every-where. The bevies of chiffchaffs and willow wrens which came to the thickets in the furze, the chorus of thrushes and blackbirds, the chaffinches in the elms, the green-finches in the hedges, wood-pigeons and turtle-doves in the copses, tree-pipits about the oaks in the cornfields; every bush, every tree, almost every clod, for the larks were so many, seemed to have its songster. As for night-ingales, I never knew so many in the most secluded country.

There are more round about London than in all the woodlands I used to ramble through. When people go into the country they really leave the birds behind them. It was the same, I found, after longer observation, with birds perhaps less widely known as with those universally recognized—such, for instance, as shrikes. The winter when the cry was raised that there were no birds, that the blackbirds and thrushes had left the lawns and must be dead, and how wicked it would be to take a nest next year, I had not the least difficulty in finding plenty of them.

They had simply gone to the water meadows, the brooks, and moist places generally. Every locality where running water kept the ground moist and permitted of movement among the creeping things which form these birds' food, was naturally resorted to. Thrushes and black-birds, although they do not pack—that is, regularly fly in flocks—undoubtedly migrate when pressed by weather.

They are well known to arrive on the east coast from Norway in numbers as the cold increases. I see no reason why we may not suppose that in very severe and con-tinued frost the thrushes and blackbirds round London fly westwards towards the milder side of the island. It seems to me that when, some years since, I used to stroll round the water meadows in a western county for snipes in frosty weather, the hedges were full of thrushes and blackbirds—quite full of them.

Now, though there were thrushes and blackbirds about

the brooks by London last winter, there were few in the hedges generally. Had they, then, flown westwards? It is my belief that they had. They had left the hard-bound ground about London for the softer and moister lands farther west. They had crossed the rain-line. When frost prevents access to food in the east, thrushes and blackbirds move westwards, just as the fieldfares and redwings do.

That the fieldfares and redwings do so I can say with confidence, because, as they move in large flocks, there is no difficulty in tracing the direction in which they are going. They all went west when the severe weather began. On the southern side of London, at least in the districts I am best acquainted with, there was hardly a fieldfare or redwing to be seen for weeks and even months. Towards spring they came back, flying east for Norway. As thrushes and blackbirds move singly, and not with concerted action, their motions cannot be determined with such precision, but all the facts are in favour of the belief that they also went west.

That they were killed by the frost and snow I utterly refuse to credit. Some few, no doubt, were—I saw some greatly enfeebled by starvation—but not the mass. If so many had been destroyed their bodies must have been seen when there was no foliage to hide them, and no insects quickly to play the scavenger as in summer. Some were killed by cats; a few perhaps by rats, for in sharp winters they go down into the ditches, and I saw a dead redwing, torn and disfigured, at the mouth of a drain during the snow, where it might have been fastened on by a rat. But it is quite improbable that thousands died as was supposed.

Thrushes and blackbirds are not like rooks. Rooks are so bound by tradition and habit that they very rarely quit the locality where they were reared. Their whole lives are spent in the neighbourhood of the nest, trees, and the woods where they sleep. They may travel miles during the day, but they always come back to roost. These are the birds that suffer the most during long frosts and snows. Unable to break the chain that binds them to one spot, they die rather than desert it. A miserable time, indeed, they had of it that winter, but I never heard that any one proposed feeding the rooks, the very birds that wanted it most.

Swallows, again, were declared by many to be fewer. It is not at all unlikely that they were fewer. The wet season was unfavourable to them; still a good deal of the supposed absence of swallows may be through the observer not looking for them in the right place. If not wheeling in the sky, look for them over the water, the river, or great ponds; if not there, look along the moist fields or shady woodland meadows. They vary their haunts with the state of the atmosphere, which causes insects to be more numerous in one place at one time, and presently in another.

A very wet season is more fatal than the sharpest frost; it acts by practically reducing the births, leaving the ordinary death-rate to continue. Consequently, as the old birds die, there are none (or fewer) to supply their places. . . .

Upon approaching the rising ground at Ewell green plovers and peewits become plentiful in the cornfields. In spring and early summer the flocks break up to some extent, and the scattered parties conduct their nesting operations in the pastures or on the downs. In autumn they collect together again, and flocks of fifty or more are commonly seen. Now and then a much larger flock comes down into the plain, wheeling to and fro, and presently descending upon an arable field, where they cover the ground.

12

A London Trout

THE SWORD-FLAGS ARE RUSTING AT THEIR EDGES, and their sharp points are turned. On the matted and entangled sedges lie the scattered leaves which every rush of the October wind hurries from the boughs. Some fall on the water and float slowly with the current, brown and yellow spots on the dark surface. The grey willows bend to the breeze; soon the osier beds will look reddish as the wands are stripped by the gusts. Alone the thick polled alders remain green, and in their shadow the brook is still darker. Through a poplar's thin branches the wind sounds as in the rigging of a ship; for the rest, it is silence.

The thrushes have not forgotten the frost of the morning, and will not sing at noon; the summer visitors have flown, and the moorhens feed quietly. The plantation by the brook is silent, for the sedges, though they have drooped and become entangled, are not dry and sapless yet to rustle loudly. They will rustle dry enough next spring, when the sedge-birds come. A long withey-bed borders the brook, and is more resorted to by sedge-reedlings, or sedge-birds, as they are variously called, than any place I know, even in the remotest country.

Generally it has been difficult to see them, because the withey is in leaf when they come, and the leaves and sheaves of innumerable rods hide them, while the ground beneath is covered by a thick growth of sedges and flags, to which the birds descend. It happened once, however, that the withey stoles had been polled, and in the spring the boughs were short and small. At the same time, the easterly winds checked the sedges, so that they were hardly half their height, and the flags were thin, and not much taller, when the sedge-birds came, so that they for once found but little cover, and could be seen to advantage.

There could not have been less than fifteen in the plantation, two frequented some bushes beside a pond near by, some stayed in scattered willows farther down the stream. They sang so much they scarcely seemed to have time to feed. While approaching one that was singing by gently walking on the sward by the road-side, or where thick dust deadened the footsteps, suddenly another would begin in the low thorn hedge on a branch, so near that it could be touched with a walking stick. Yet though so near the bird was not wholly visible—he was partly concealed behind a fork of the bough. This is a habit of the sedge-birds. Not in the least timid, they chatter at your elbow, and yet always partially hidden.

If in the withey, they choose a spot where the rods cross or bunch together. If in the sedges, though so close it seems as if you could reach forward and catch him, he is behind the stalks. To place some obstruction between themselves and any one passing is their custom; but that spring, as the foliage was so thin, it only needed a little dexterity in peering to get a view. The sedge-bird perches aside, on a sloping willow rod, and, slightly raising his head, chatters, turning his bill from side to side. He is a very tiny bird, and his little eye looks out from under a yellowish streak. His song at first sounds nothing but chatter.

After listening a while the ear finds a scale in it—an arrangement and composition—so that, though still a chatter, it is a tasteful one. At intervals he intersperses a chirp, exactly the same as that of the sparrow, a chirp with a tang in it. Strike a piece of metal, and besides the noise of the blow, there is a second note, or tang. The sparrow's chirp has such a note sometimes, and the sedge-bird brings it in—tang, tang, tang. This sound has given him his country name of brook-sparrow, and it rather spoils his song. Often the moment he has concluded he starts for another willow stole, and as he flies begins to chatter when halfway across, and finishes on a fresh branch.

But long before this another bird has begun to sing in a bush adjacent; a third takes it up in the thorn hedge; a fourth in the bushes across the pond; and from farther down the stream comes a faint and distant chatter. Ceaselessly the competing gossip goes on the entire day and most of the night; indeed, sometimes all night through. On a warm spring morning, when the sunshine pours upon the willows, and even the white dust of the road is brighter, bringing out the shadows in clear definition, their lively notes and quick motions make a pleasant commentary on the low sound of the stream rolling round the curve.

A moorhen's call comes from the hatch. Broad yellow petals of marsh-marigold stand up high among the sedges rising from the greyish-green ground, which is covered with a film of sun-dried aquatic grass left dry by the retiring waters. Here and there are lilac-tinted cuckoo-flowers, drawn up on taller stalks than those that grow in the meadows. The black flowers of the sedges are powdered with yellow pollen; and dark green sword-flags are beginning to spread their fans. But just across the road, on the topmost twigs of birch poles, swallows twitter in the tenderest tones to their loves. From the oaks in the meadows on that side titlarks mount above the highest bough and then descend, sing, sing, singing, to the grass.

A jay calls in a circular copse in the midst of the
meadow; solitary rooks go over to their nests in the elms
on the hill; cuckoos call, now this way and now that, as
they travel round. While leaning on the grey and lichen-
hung rails by the brook, the current glides by, and it is
the motion of the water and its low murmur which renders
the place so idle; the sunbeams brood, the air is still but
full of song. Let us, too, stay and watch the petals fall
one by one from a wild apple and float down on the stream.

But now in autumn the haws are red on the thorn,
the swallows are few as they were in the earliest spring;
the sedge-birds have flown, and the redwings will soon
be here. The sharp points of the sword-flags are turned,
their edges rusty, the forget-me-nots are gone. October's
winds are too searching for us to linger beside the brook,
but still it is pleasant to pass by and remember the summer
days. For the year is never gone by; in a moment we can
recall the sunshine we enjoyed in May, the roses we
gathered in June, the first wheatear we plucked as the green
corn filled. Other events go by and are forgotten, and
even the details of our own lives, so immensely important
to us at the moment, in time fade from the memory till
the date we fancied we should never forget has to be
sought in a diary. But the year is always with us; the
months are familiar always; they have never gone by.

So with the red haws around and the rustling leaves it
is easy to recall the flowers. The withey plantation here
is full of flowers in summer; yellow iris flowers in June
when midsummer comes, for the iris loves a thunder-
shower. The flowering flag spreads like a fan from the
root, the edges overlap near the ground, and the leaves
are broad as sword-blades, indeed the plant is one of the
largest that grows wild. It is quite different from the
common flag with three grooves—bayonet shape—which

appears in every brook. The yellow iris is much more local, and in many countries streams may be sought for in vain, so that so fine a display as may be seen here seemed almost a discovery to me. . . .

There is a beech in the plantation standing so near the verge of the stream that its boughs droop over. It has a number of twigs around the stem—as a rule the beech-bole is clear of boughs, but some which are of rather stunted growth are fringed with them. The leaves on the longer boughs above fall off and voyage down the brook, but those on the lesser twigs beneath, and only a little way from the ground, remain on, and rustle, dry and brown, all through the winter.

Under the shelter of these leaves, and close to the trunk, there grew a plant of flag—the tops of the flags almost reached to the leaves—and all the winter through, despite the frosts for which it was remarkable, despite the snow and the bitter winds which followed, this plant remained green and fresh. From this beech in the morning a shadow stretches to a bridge across the brook, and in that shadow my trout used to lie. The bank under the drooping boughs forms a tiny cliff a foot high, covered with moss, and here I once observed shrew mice diving and racing about. But only once, though I frequently passed the spot; it is curious that I did not see them afterwards.

Just below the shadow of the beech there is a sandy, oozy shore, where the footprints of moorhens are often traceable. Many of the trees of the plantation stand in water after heavy rain; their leaves drop into it in autumn, and, being away from the influence of the current, stay and soak, and lie several layers thick. Their edges overlap, red, brown, and pale yellow, with the clear water above and shadows athwart it, and dry white grass at the verge.

A horse-chestnut drops its fruit in the dusty road; high above its leaves are tinted with scarlet.

It was at the tail of one of the arches of the bridge over the brook that my favourite trout used to lie. Sometimes the shadow of the beech came as far as his haunts, that was early in the morning, and for the rest of the day the bridge itself cast a shadow. The other parapet faces the south, and looking down from it the bottom of the brook is generally visible, because the light is so strong. At the bottom a green plant may be seen waving to and fro in summer as the current sways it. It is not a weed or flag, but a plant with pale green leaves, and looks as if it had come there by some chance; this is the water-parsnip.

By the shore on this, the sunny side of the bridge, a few forget-me-nots grow in their season, water crow's-foot flowers, flags lie along the surface and slowly swing from side to side like a boat at anchor. The breeze brings a ripple, and the sunlight sparkles on it; the light reflected dances up the piers of the bridge. Those that pass along the road are naturally drawn to this bright parapet where the brook winds brimming full through green meadows. You can see right to the bottom; you can see where the rush of the water has scooped out a deeper channel under the arches, but look as long as you like there are no fish.

The trout I watched so long, and with such pleasure, was always on the other side, at the tail of the arch, waiting for whatever might come through to him. There in perpetual shadow he lay in wait, a little at the side of the arch, scarcely ever varying his position except to dart a yard up under the bridge to seize anything he fancied, and drifting out again to bring up at his anchorage. If people looked over the parapet that side they did not see him; they could not see the bottom there for the shadow, or if the summer noonday cast a strong beam even then it seemed to cover the surface of the water with a film of light which could not be seen through. There are some aspects from which even a picture hung on the wall close at hand cannot be seen. So no one saw the trout; if any one more curious leant over the parapet he was gone in a moment under the arch.

Folk fished in the pond about the verge of which the sedge-birds chattered, and but a few yards distant; but they never looked under the arch on the northern and shadowy side, where the water flowed beside the beech. For three seasons this continued. For three summers I had the pleasure to see the trout day after day whenever I walked that way, and all that time, with fishermen close at hand, he escaped notice, though the place was not preserved. It is wonderful to think how difficult it is to see anything under one's very eyes, and thousands of people walked actually and physically right over the fish.

However, one morning in the third summer, I found a fisherman standing in the road and fishing over the parapet in the shadowy water. But he was fishing at the wrong arch, and only with paste for roach. While the man stood there fishing, along came two navvies; naturally enough they went quietly up to see what the fisherman was doing, and one instantly uttered an exclamation. He had seen the trout. The man who was fishing with paste, had stood so still and patient that the trout, reassured, had come out, and the navvy—trust a navvy to see anything of the kind—caught sight of him.

The navvy knew how to see through water. He told the fisherman, and there was a stir of excitement, a changing of hooks and bait. I could not stay to see the result, but went on, fearing the worst. But he did not succeed; next day the wary trout was there still, and the next, and the next. Either this particular fisherman was not able to

come again, or was discouraged; at any rate, he did not
try again. The fish escaped, doubtless more wary than
ever.

In the spring of the next year the trout was still there,
and up to the summer I used to go and glance at him.
This was the fourth season, and still he was there; I took
friends to look at this wonderful fish, which defied all
the loafers and poachers, and above all, surrounded himself not only with the shadow of the bridge, but threw
a mental shadow over the minds of passers-by, so that
they never thought of the possibility of such a thing as
trout. But one morning something happened. The brook
was dammed up on the sunny side of the bridge, and the
water let off by a side-hatch, that some accursed main or
pipe or other horror might be laid across the bed of the
stream somewhere far down.

Above the bridge there was a brimming broad brook,
below it the flags lay on the mud, the weeds drooped, and
the channel was dry. It was dry up to the beech tree. There,
under the drooping boughs of the beech, was a small pool
of muddy water, perhaps two yards long, and very narrow
—a stagnant muddy pool, not more than three or four
inches deep. In this I saw the trout. In the shallow water,
his back came up to the surface (for his fins must have
touched the mud sometimes)—once it came above the
surface, and his spots showed as plain as if you had held
him in your hand. He was swimming round to try to
find out the reason of this sudden stinting of room.

Twice he heaved himself somewhat on his side over
a dead branch that was at the bottom, and exhibited all
his beauty to the air and sunshine. Then he went away
into another part of the shallow and was hidden by the
muddy water. Now under the arch of the bridge, his
favourite arch, close by there was a deep pool, for, as

G

already mentioned, the scour of the current scooped away the sand and made a hole there. When the stream was shut off by the dam above this hole remained partly full. Between this pool and the shallow under the beech there was sufficient connection for the fish to move into it.

My only hope was that he would do so, and as some showers fell, temporarily increasing the depth of the narrow canal between the two pools, there seemed every reason to believe that he had got to that under the arch. If now only that accursed pipe or main, or whatever repair it was, could only be finished quickly, even now the trout might escape! Every day my anxiety increased, for the intelligence would soon get about that the brook was dammed up, and any pools left in it would be sure to attract attention.

Sunday came, and directly the bells had done ringing four men attacked the pool under the arch. They took off shoes and stockings and waded in, two at each end of the arch. Stuck in the mud close by was an eel-spear. They churned up the mud, wading in, and thickened and darkened it as they groped under. No one could watch these barbarians longer.

Is it possible that he could have escaped? He was a wonderful fish, wary and quick. Is it just possible that they may not even have known that a trout was there at all; but have merely hoped for perch, or tench, or eels? The pool was deep and the fish quick—they did not bale it, might he have escaped? Might they even, if they did find him, have mercifully taken him and placed him alive in some other water nearer their homes? Is it possible that he may have almost miraculously made his way down the stream into other pools?

There was very heavy rain one night, which might have given him such a chance. These "mights", and "ifs", and "is it possible" even now keep alive some little hope that some day I may yet see him again. But that was in the early summer. It is now winter, and the beech has brown spots. Among the limes the sedges are matted and entangled, the sword-flags rusty; the rooks are at the acorns, and the plough is at work in the stubble. I have never seen him since. I never failed to glance over the parapet into the shadowy water. Somehow it seemed to look colder, darker, less pleasant than it used to do. The spot was empty, and the shrill winds whistled through the poplars.

13

The Coming of Summer Near London

THE JUNE SKY IS OF THE DEEPEST BLUE WHEN SEEN above the fresh foliage of the oaks in the morning before the sun has filled the heavens with his meridian light. To see the blue at its best it needs something to form a screen so that the azure may strike the eye with its fulness undiminished by its own beauty; for if you look at the open sky such a breadth of the same hue tones itself down. But let the eye rise upwards along a wall of oak spray, then at the rim the rich blue is thick, quite thick, opaque, and steeped in luscious colour. Unless, indeed, upon the high downs,—there the June sky is too deep even for the brilliance of the light, and requires no more screen than the hand put up to shade the eyes. These level plains by the Thames are different, and here I like to see the sky behind and over an oak.

About Surbiton the oaks come out into leaf earlier than in many places; this spring [1881] there were oak-leaves appearing on April 24, yet so backward are some of them that, while all the rest were green, there were two in the hedge of a field by the Ewell road still dark within ten days of June. They looked dark because their trunks and boughs were leafless against a background of hawthorn, elm, and other trees in full foliage, the clover flowering under them, and May bloom on the hedge.

They were black as winter, and even now, on the 1st of June, the leaves are not fully formed.

St. Mary Aldermanbury
Church

The trees flowered in great perfection this spring; many oaks were covered with their green pendants, and they hung from the sycamores. Except the chestnuts, whose bloom can scarcely be overlooked, the flowering of the trees is but little noticed; the elm is one of the earliest, and becomes ruddy—it is as early as the catkins on the hazel; willow, aspen, oak, sycamore, ash, all have flower or catkin—even the pine, whose fructification is very interesting. The pines or Scotch firs by the Long Ditton road hang their sweeping branches to the verge of the footpath, and the new cones, the sulphur farina, and the fresh shoots are easily seen. The very earliest oak to put forth its flowers is in a garden on Oak Hill; it is green with them, while yet the bitter winds have left a sense of winter in the air.

There is a broad streak of bright-yellow charlock— in the open arable field beyond the Common. It lights up the level landscape; the glance falls on it immediately. Field beans are in flower, and their scent comes sweet even through the dust of the Derby Day. Red heads of trifolium dot the ground; the vetches have long since been out, and are so still; along the hedges parsley forms a white fringe. The charlock seems late this year; it is generally well before June—the first flowers by the roadside or rickyard, in a waste dry corner. Such dry waste places send up plants to flower, such as charlock and poppy, quicker than happens in better soil, but they do not reach nearly the height or size. The field beans are short from lack of rain; there are some reeds in the ditch by them, and these too are short; they have not half shot up yet, for the same reason. On the sward by the Long Ditton road the goat's-beard is up; it grows to some size there every season, but is not very common elsewhere. It is said to close its sepals at noon, and was therefore called "Jack-go-bed-at-noon", but in fact it shuts much earlier, and often does not open at all, and you may pass twenty times and not see it open. Its head is like that of the dandelion, and children blow it to see what's o'clock in the same way. It forms a large ball, and browner; dandelion seed-balls are white. The grass is dotted with them now; they give a glossy, silky appearance to the meadows. Tiny pink geranium flowers show on bunches of dusty grass; silver weed lays its yellow buttercup-like flower on the ground, placing it in the angle of the road and the sward, where the sward makes a ridge. Cockspur grass—three claws and a spur like a cock's-foot—is already whitened with pollen; already in comparison, for the grasses are late to lift their heads this summer. As the petals of the May fall the young leaves appear, small and green, gradually to enlarge through the hay-time.

A slight movement of the leaves on a branch of birch shows that something living is there, and presently the little head and neck of a whitethroat peers over them, and then under, looking above and beneath each leaf, and then with a noiseless motion passing on to the next. Another whitethroat follows immediately, and there is not a leaf forgotten nor a creeping thing that can hide from them. Every tree and every bush is visited by these birds, and others of the insect-feeders; the whole summer's day they are searching, and the caterpillar, as it comes down on a thread, slipping from the upper branches, only drops into their beaks. Birds, too, that at other periods feed on grain and seed, now live themselves, and bring up their young, upon insects.

I went to look over a gate to see how the corn was rising—it is so short, now in June, that it will not hide a hare—and on coming near there was a cock chaffinch perched on the top, a fine bird in full colour. He did not move though I was now within three yards, nor till I could have almost touched him did he fly; he had a large cater-pillar in his beak, and no doubt his nest or the young from it were in the hedge. In feeding the young birds the old ones always perch first at a short distance, and after wait-ing a minute proceed to their fledgelings. Should a blackbird come at full speed across the meadow and stay on a hedge-top, and then go down into the mound, it is certain that his nest is there. If a thrush frequents a tree, flying up into the branches for a minute, and then descending into the underwood, most likely the young thrushes are there.

Little indeed do the birds care for appropriate sur-roundings; anything does for them, they do not aim at effect. I heard a tit-lark singing his loudest, and found him perched on the edge of a tub, formed of a barrel sawn in two, placed in the field for the horses to drink from, as there was no pond. Some swallows are very fond of a notice-board fastened to a pole beside the Hogsmill bank. Upon its upper edge they perch and twitter sweetly. There is a muddy pond by Tolworth Farm, near the road; it is muddy because a herd of cows drink from and stand in it, stirring up the bottom. An elm overhangs it, and the lower boughs are dead and leafless. On these there are always swallows twittering over the water. Grey and yellow wagtails run along the verge. In the morning the flock of goslings who began to swim in the pond, now grown large and grey, arrange themselves in a double row, some twenty or thirty of them, in loose order, tuck their bills under their wings and sleep. Two old birds stand in the rear as if in command of the detachment. A sow, plastered with mud like the rhinoceri in the African lakes, lies on the edge of the brown water, so nearly the hue of the water and the mire, and so exactly at their juncture, as to be easily overlooked. But the sweet summer swallows sing on the branches; they do not see the wallowing animal, they see only the sunshine and the summer, golden buttercups and blue sky.

In the hollow at Long Ditton I had the delight, a day or two since, to see a kingfisher. There is a quiet lane, and at the bottom, in a valley, two ponds, one in enclosed grounds, the other in a meadow opposite. . . . Standing there a minute to see if there was a martin among the birds with which the pond in the grounds is thickly covered, something came shooting straight towards me, and swerving only a yard or two to pass me, a kingfisher went by. His blue wings, his ruddy front, the white streak beside his neck, and long bill, were all visible for a moment; then he was away straight over the meadow, the directness of his course enabling it to be followed for some time till he cleared the distant hedge, probably going to visit his nest. Kingfishers, though living by the stream, often build a good way from water. The months have lengthened into years since I saw one here before, sitting on the trunk of a willow which bends over the pond in the mead. The tree rises out of the water and is partly in it; it is hung with moss, and the kingfisher was on the trunk within a foot or so of the surface. After that there came severe winters, and till now I did not see another here. So that the bird came upon me unexpectedly out from the shadow of the trees that overhang the water, past me, and on into the sunshine over the buttercups and sorrel of the field.

This hollow at Long Ditton is the very place of singing birds; never was such a place for singing—the valley is full of music. In the oaks blackbirds whistle. You do not often see them; they are concealed by the thick foliage up on high, for they seek the top branches, which are more leafy; but once now and then they flutter quietly

across to another perch. The blackbird's whistle is very
human, like a human being playing the flute; an uncertain
player, now drawing forth a bar of a beautiful melody
and then losing it again. He does not know what quiver
or what turn his note will take before it ends; the note
leads him and completes itself. It is a song which strives
to express the singer's keen delight, the singer's exquisite
appreciation of the loveliness of the days; the golden glory
of the meadow, the light, the luxurious shadows, the indolent clouds reclining on their azure couch. Such thoughts
can only be expressed in fragments, like a sculptor's chips
thrown off as the inspiration seizes him, not mechanically
sawn to a set line. Now and again the blackbird feels the
beauty of the time, the large white daisy stars, the grass
with yellow-dusted tips, the air which comes so softly
unperceived by any precedent rustle of the hedge, the
water which runs slower, held awhile by rootlet, flag, and
forget-me-not. He feels the beauty of the time and he
must say it. His notes come like wild flowers, not sown in
order. The sunshine opens and shuts the stops of his
instrument. There is not an oak without a blackbird, and
there are others afar off in the hedges. The thrushes sing
louder here than anywhere; they really seem to have
louder notes; they are all round. Thrushes appear to vary
their songs with the period of the year; they sing loudly
now, but more plaintively and delicately in the autumn.
Warblers and willow wrens sing out of sight among the
trees; they are easily hidden by a leaf; ivy-leaves are so
smooth, with an enamelled surface, that high up, as the
wind moves them, they reflect the sunlight and scintillate.
Greenfinches in the elms never cease love-making, and
love-making needs much soft talking. There is a nightingale in a bush by the lane which sings so loud the
hawthorn seems to shake with the vigour of his song;

too loud, though a nightingale, if you stand at the verge of the boughs, as he would let you without alarm; farther away it becomes sweet and softer. Yellow-hammers call from the trees up towards the arable fields. There are but a few of them: it is the place of singing birds.

The doves in the copse are nearer the house this year; I see them more often in the field at the end of the garden. As the dove rises the white fringe on the tip of the tail becomes visible, especially when flying up into a tree. One afternoon one flew up into a hornbeam close to the garden, beside it in fact, and perched there full in view, not twenty yards at farthest. At first he sat upright, raising his neck and watching us in the garden; then, in a minute or so, turned and fluttered down to his nest. The wood-pigeons are more quiet now; their whoo-hoo-ing is not so frequently heard. By the sounds up in the elms at the top of the Brighton road (at the end of Langley Lane) the young rooks have not yet all flown, though it is the end of the first week in June. There is a little pond near the rookeries, and by it a row of elms. From one of these a heavy bough has just fallen without the least apparent cause. There is no sign of lightning, nor does it even look decayed; the wood has fractured short off; it came down with such force that the ends of the lesser branches are broken and turned up, though, as it was the lowest limb, it had not far to fall, showing the weight of the timber. There has been no hurricane of wind, nothing at all to cause it, yet this thick bough snapped. No other tree is subject to these dangerous falls of immense limbs, without warning or apparent cause, so that it is not safe to rest under elms. An accident might not occur once in ten years; nevertheless the risk is there. Elms topple over before gales which scarcely affect other trees, or only tear off a few twigs. Two have thus been thrown recently—

within eighteen months—in the fields opposite Tolworth Farm. The elm drags up its own roots, which are often only a fringe round its butt, and leaves a hollow in the earth, as if it had been simply stood on end and held by these guy-ropes. Other trees do, indeed, fall in course of time, but not till they are obviously on the point of tottering, but the elm goes down in full pride of foliage. By this pond there is a rough old oak, which is the peculiar home of some titmice; they were there every day, far back on the frost and snow, and their sharp notes sounded like some one chipping the ice on the horse-pond with an iron instrument. Probably, before now, they have had a nest in a crevice.

The tallest grass yet to be seen is in a little orchard on the right-hand side of the Long Ditton road. This little orchard is a favourite spot of mine, meaning, of course, to look at; it is a natural orchard and left to itself. The palings by the road are falling, and held up chiefly by the brambles and the ivy that has climbed up them. There are trees on the left and trees on the right; a fine spruce fir at the back. The apple-trees are not set in straight lines; they were at first, but some have died away and left an irregularity. The trees themselves lean this way and that; they are scarred and marked, as it were, with lichen and moss. It is the home of birds. A blackbird had a nest this spring in the bushes on the left side, a nightingale in the bushes on the right side, and there he sang and sang for hours every morning. A sharp, relentless shrike lives in one of the trees close by, and is perpetually darting across the road upon insects on the sward among the fern there. There are several thrushes who reside in this orchard beside the lesser birds. Swallows sometimes twitter from the tops of the apple-trees. As the grass is so safe from intrusion, one of the earliest buttercups flowers here. The apple-bloom appears rosy on the bare boughs only lately scourged by the east wind. After a time the trees are in full bloom, set about into the green of the hedges and bushes and the dark spruce behind. Bennets, the flower of the grass, come up. The first bennet is to green things what a swallow is to the breathing creatures of summer. White horse-chestnut blooms stand up in their stately way, lighting the path, which is strewn with fallen oak-flower. May appears on the hawthorn: there is an early bush of it. Now the grass is so high the flowers are lost under it; even the buttercups are overtopped; and soon as the young apples take form and shape white bramble-bloom will cover the bushes by the palings. Acorns will show on the oaks: the berries will ripen from red to black beneath. Along the edge of the path, where the dandelions and plantains are thick with seed, the greenfinches will come down and select those they like best: this they often do by the footpath beside the road. Lastly, the apples become red; the beech in the corner has an orange spray, and cones hang long and brown upon the spruce. The thrushes after silence sing again, and autumn approaches. But, pass when you may, this little orchard has always something, because it is left to itself—I had written neglected. I struck the word out, for this is not neglect, this is true attention, to leave it to itself, so that the young trees trail over the bushes and stay till the berries fall of their own over-ripeness, if perchance spared by the birds; so that the dead brown leaves lie and are not swept away unless the wind pleases; so that all things follow their own course and bent. Almost opposite, by autumn, when the reapers are busy with the sheaves, the hedge is white with the large trumpet-flowers of the greater convolvulus. The hedgerow seems made of convolvulus then, nothing but convolvulus; nowhere else does the flower flourish so strongly, and the bines remain until the following spring. This little orchard, without a path through it, without a border, or a parterre, or a terrace, is a place to sit down and dream in, notwithstanding that it touches the road, for thus left to itself it has acquired an atmosphere of peace and stillness such as belongs to and grows up in woods and far-away coombs of the hills. A stray passer-by would go on without even noticing it, it is so commonplace and unpretentious, merely a corner of meadow irregularly dotted with apple-trees; a place that needs frequent glances and a dreamy mood to understand as the birds understand it. They are always here, even in the winter, starlings and blackbirds particularly, who resort to a kind of furrow there, which, even in frost, seems to afford them some food. In the spring thrushes move along, rustling the fallen leaves as they search behind the arum-sheaths unrolling beside the palings, or under the shelter of the group of trees where arum-roots are plentiful. There are nooks and corners from which shy creatures can steal out from the shadow and be happy. The dew falls softly, more noiseless than snow, and a star shines to the north over the spruce fir. By day there is a loving streak of sunshine somewhere among the tree-trunks; by night a star above. The trees are nothing to speak of in size or height, but they seem always to bloom well and to be fruitful; tree-climbers run up these and then go off to the elms.

Beside the Long Ditton road, up the gentle incline on the left side, the broad sward is broken by thickets and brake like those of a forest. If a forest were cleared, as those in America are swept away before the axe, but a line of underwood left beside the highway, the result would be much the same as may be seen here when the bushes and fern are in perfection. Thick hawthorn bushes stand at unequal distances surrounded with brake; one with a young oak in the centre. Fern extends from one thicket to the other, and brambles fence the thorns, which are themselves well around. From such coverts the boar was started in old English days, the fawns hide behind and about them even now in many a fair park, and where there are no deer they are frequented by hares. So near the dust which settles on them as the wheels raise it, of course, every dog that passes runs through, and no game could stay an hour, but they are the exact kind of cover game like. One morning this spring, indeed, I noticed a cock-pheasant calmly walking along the ridge of a furrow in the ploughed field, parted from these bushes by the hedge. He was so near the highway that I could see the ring about his neck. I have seen peewits or green plovers in the same field, which is now about to be built on. But though no game could stay an hour in such places, lesser birds love them, whitethroats build there, gold-crests come down from the dark pines opposite—they seem fond of pines—yellow-hammers sit and sing on them, and they are visited all day long by one or other. The little yellow flowers of tormentil are common in the grass as autumn approaches, and grasshoppers, which do not seem plentiful here, sing there. Some betony flowers are opposite on the other sward. There is a marshy spot by one of the bushes where among the rushes various semi-aquatic grasses grow. Blackberries are thick in favourable seasons —like all fruit, they are an uncertain crop; and hawk-weeds are there everywhere on the sward towards the edge. The peculiar green of fern, which is more of a relief to the eye than any other shrub with which I am acquainted, so much so that I wonder it is not more imitated, is re-markable here when the burning July sun shines on the white dust thus fringed. By then trees are gone off in colour, the hedges are tired with heat, but the fern is a soft green which holds the glance. This varies much with various seasons; this year the fern is particularly late from a lack of moisture, but sometimes it is really beautiful between these bushes. . . .

In the evening from the rise of the road here I sometimes hear the cry of a barn owl skirting the hedge of Southborough Park, and disappearing under the shadow of the elms that stand there. The stars appear and the whole dome of the summer night is visible, for in a level plain like this a slight elevation brings the horizon into view. Without moon the June nights are white; a faint white light shows through the trees of Southborough Park northwards; the west has not lost all its tint over the Ditton hollow; white flowers stand in the grass; white road, white flint-heaps even, white clouds, and the stars, too, light without colour.

By day the breeze comes south and west, free over fields, over corn and grass and hedgerow; so slight a mound as this mere rise in the river-side plain lifts you up into the current of the air. Where the wind comes the sunlight is purer.

The sorrel is now high and ripening in the little meadows beside the road just beyond the orchard. As it ripens the meadow becomes red, for the stalks rise above the grass. This is the beginning of the feast of seeds. The sorrel ripens just as the fledgelings are leaving the nest; if you watch the meadow a minute you will see the birds go out to it, now flying up a moment and then settling again. After a while comes the feast of grain; then another feast of seeds among the stubble, and the ample fields, and the furze of the hills; then berries, and then winter, and the last seed.

A June rose. Something caught my eye on the top of the high hawthorn hedge beside the Brighton road one evening as it was growing dusk, and on looking again there was a spray of briar in flower, two roses in full bloom and out of reach, and one spray of three growing buds. So it is ever with the June rose. It is found unexpectedly, and when you are not looking for it. It is a gift, not a discovery, or anything earned—a gift like love and happiness. With ripening grasses the rose comes, and the rose is summer: till then it is spring. On the green banks—waste places—beside the "New Road" (Kingsdown Road formerly) the streaked pink convolvulus is in flower; a sign that the spring forces have spent themselves, that the sun is near his fulness. The flower itself is shapely, yet it is not quite welcome; it says too plainly that we are near the meridian. There are months of warmth to follow—brilliant sunshine and new beauties; but the freshness, the joyous looking forward of spring is gone. Upon these banks the first coltsfoot flowers in March, the first convolvulus in summer, and almost the last hawkweed in autumn. A yellow vetchling, too, is not opening its yellow petals beside the Long Ditton road: another summer flower, which comes in as the blue veronica is leaving the grass.

As tall as the young corn the may weed fringes the arable fields with its white rays and yellow centre, somewhat as the broad moon-daisies stand in the grass. By this time generally the corn is high above the mayweed, but this year the flower is level with its shelter. The pale corn buttercup is in flower by the New Road, not in the least overshadowed by the crops at the edge of which it grows. By the stream through Tolworth Common spotted persicaria is rising thickly, but even this strong-growing plant is backward and checked on the verge of the shrunken stream. The showers that have since fallen have not made up for the lack of the April rains, which in the most literal sense cause the flowers of May and June. Without those early spring rains the wild flowers cannot push their roots and develop their stalks in time for the summer sun. The sunshine and heat finds them unprepared. In the ditches the square-stemmed figwort is conspicuous by its dark green. It is very plentiful about Surbiton. Just outside the garden in a waste corner the yellow flowers of celandine are over-hung by wild hops and white bryony, two strong plants of which have climbed up the copse hedge, twining in and out each other. Both have vine-like leaves; but the hops are wrinkled, those of the bryony hairy or rough to the touch. The hops seem to be the most powerful, and hold the bryony in the background. The young spruce firs which the wood-pigeon visited in the spring with an idea of building there look larger and thicker now the fresh green needles have appeared.

In the woodland lane to Claygate the great elder-bushes are coming into flower, each petal a creamy-white. The dogwood, too, is opening, and the wild guelder-roses there are in full bloom. There is a stile from which a path leads across the fields thence to Hook. The field by the stile was fed off in spring, and now is yellow with birds-foot lotus, which tints it because the grass is so short. From the grass at every footstep a crowd of little "hoppers" leap in every direction, scattering themselves hastily abroad. The little mead by the copse here is more open to the view this year, as the dry winter has checked the growth of ferns and rushes. There is a flock of missel-thrushes in it: the old birds feed the young, who can fly well in the centre of the field. Lesser birds come over from the hedges to the bunches of rushes. Slowly wandering along the lane and looking over the mound on the right hand (cow-wheat with yellow lip is in flower on the mound), there are glimpses between the bushes and the Spanish chestnut-trees of far-away blue hills—blue under the summer sky.

H

14

Herbs at Kew Gardens

A GREAT GREEN BOOK, WHOSE BROAD PAGES ARE illuminated with flowers, lies open at the feet of Londoners. This volume, without further preface, lies ever open at Kew Gardens, and is most easily accessible from every part of the metropolis. A short walk from Kew station brings the visitor to Cumberland Gate. Resting for a moment upon the first seat that presents itself, it is hard to realize that London has but just been quitted.

Green foliage around, green grass beneath, a pleasant sensation—not silence, but absence of jarring sound—blue sky overhead, streaks and patches of sunshine where the branches admit the rays, wide, cool shadows, and clear, sweet atmosphere. High in a lime tree, hidden from view by the leaves, a chiffchaff sings continually, and from the distance comes the softer note of a thrush. On the close-mown grass a hedge-sparrow is searching about within a few yards, and idle insects float to and fro, visible against the background of a dark yew tree—they could not be seen in the glare of the sunshine. The peace of green things reigns.

It is not necessary to go farther in; this spot at the very entrance is equally calm and still, for there is no margin of partial disturbance—repose begins at the edge. Perhaps it is best to be at once content, and to move no farther; to remain, like the lime tree, in one spot, with the sunshine and the sky, to close the eyes and listen to the thrush. Something, however, urges exploration.

The majority of visitors naturally follow the path, and go round into the general expanse; but I will turn from here sharply to the right, and crossing the sward there is, after a few steps only, another enclosing wall. Within this enclosure, called the Herbaceous Ground, heedlessly passed and perhaps never heard of by the thousands who go to see the Palm Houses, lies to me the real and truest interest of Kew. For here is a living dictionary of English wild flowers.

The meadow and the cornfield, the river, the mountain and the woodland, the seashore, the very waste place by the roadside, each has sent its peculiar representatives, and glancing for the moment, at large, over the beds, noting their number and extent, remembering that the specimens are not in the mass but individual, the first conclusion is that our own country is the true Flowery Land.

But the immediate value of this wonderful garden is in the clue it gives to the most ignorant, enabling any one, no matter how unlearned, to identify the flower that delighted him or her, it may be, years ago, in far-away field or copse. Walking up and down the green paths between the beds, you are sure to come upon it presently, with its scientific name duly attached and its natural order labelled at the end of the patch.

Had I only known of this place in former days how gladly I would have walked the hundred miles hither! For the old folk, the aged men and countrywomen, have for the most part forgotten, if they ever knew, the plants and herbs in the hedges they had frequented from child-hood. Some few, of course, they can tell you; but the majority are as unknown to them, except by sight, as the ferns of New Zealand or the heaths of the Cape.

Since books came about, since the railways and science

destroyed superstition, the lore of herbs has in great measure decayed and been lost. The names of many of the commonest herbs are quite forgotten—they are weeds, and nothing more. But here these things are preserved; in London, the centre of civilization and science, is a garden which restores the ancient knowledge of the monks and the witches of the villages.

Thus, on entering to-day, the first plant which I observed is hellebore—a not very common wild herb perhaps, but found in places, and a traditionary use of which is still talked of in the country. What would the sturdy mowers whom I once watched cutting their way steadily through the tall grass in June say, could they see here the black knapweed cultivated as a garden treasure? Its hard woody head with purple florets lifted high above the ground, was greatly disliked by them, as, too, the blue scabious, and indeed most other flowers. The stalks of such plants were so much harder to mow than the grass.

Feathery yarrow sprays, which spring up by the wayside and wherever the foot of man passes, as at the gateway, are here. White and lilac-tinted yarrow flowers grow so thickly along the roads round London as often to form a border between the footpath and the bushes of the hedge. Dandelions lift their yellow heads, classified and cultivated—the same dandelions whose brilliant colour is admired and imitated by artists, and whose prepared roots are still in use in country places to improve the flavour of coffee.

Groundsel, despised groundsel, the weed which cumbers the garden patch, and is hastily destroyed, is here fully recognized. These harebells—they have flowered a little earlier than in their wild state—how many scenes they recall to memory! We found them on the tops of the glorious Downs when the wheat was ripe in the plains

and the earth beneath seemed all golden. Some, too, concealed themselves on the pastures behind those bunches
of tough grass the cattle left untouched. And even in cold
November, when the mist lifted, while the dewdrops
clustered thickly on the grass, one or two hung their
heads under the furze.

Hawkweeds, which many mistake for dandelions; cowslips, in seed now, and primroses, with foreign primulas
around them and enclosed by small hurdles, foxgloves,
some with white and some with red flowers, all these have
their story and are intensely English. Rough-leaved com-
frey of the side of the river and brook, one species of
which is so much talked of as better forage than grass, is
here, its bells opening.

Borage, whose leaves float in the claret-cup ladled out
to thirsty travellers at the London railway stations in the
hot weather; knotted figwort, common in ditches; Aaron's
rod, found in old gardens; lovely veronicas; mints and
calamints whose leaves, if touched, scent the fingers, and
which grow everywhere by cornfield and hedgerow.

This bunch of wild thyme once again calls up a vision
of the Downs; it is not so thick and strong, and it lacks
that cushion of herbage which so often marks the site
of its growth on the noble slopes of the hills, and along
the sward-grown fosse of ancient earthworks, but it is
wild thyme, and that is enough. From this bed of varieties
of thyme there rises up a pleasant odour which attracts
the bees. Bees and humble-bees, indeed, buzz everywhere,
but they are much too busily occupied to notice you or me.

Is there any difference in the taste of London honey and
in that of the country? From the immense quantity of
garden flowers about the metropolis it would seem possible
for a distinct flavour, not perhaps preferable, to be im-
parted. Lavender, of which old housewives were so fond,

and which is still the best of preservatives, comes next, and self-heal is just coming out in flower; the reapers have, I believe, forgotten its former use in curing the gashes sometimes inflicted by the reaphook. The reaping machine has banished such memories from the stubble. Nightshades border on the potato, the flowers of both almost exactly alike; poison and food growing side by side and of the same species.

There are tales still told in the villages of this deadly and enchanted mandragora; the lads sometimes go to the churchyards to search for it. Plantains and docks, wild spurge, hops climbing up a dead fir tree, a well-chosen pole for them—nothing is omitted. Even the silver weed, the dusty-looking foliage which is thrust aside as you walk on the footpath by the road is here labelled with truth as "cosmopolitan" of habit.

Bird's-foot lotus, another Downside plant, lights up the stones put to represent rockwork with its yellow. Saxifrage, and stone-crop and house-leek are here in variety. Buttercups occupy a whole patch—a little garden to themselves. What would the haymakers say to such a sight? Little, too, does the mower reck of the number, variety, and beauty of the grasses in a single armful of swathe, such as he gathers up to cover his jar of ale with and keep it cool by the hedge. The bennets, the flower of the grass, on their tall stalks, go down in numbers as countless as the sand of the seashore before his scythe.

But here the bennets are watched and tended, the weeds removed from around them, and all the grasses of the field cultivated as affectionately as the finest rose. There is something cool and pleasant in this green after the colours of the herbs in flower, though each grass is but a bunch, yet it has with it something of the sweetness of the meadows by the brooks. Juncus, the rush, is here, a sign often welcome to cattle, for they know that water must be near; the bunch is cut down, and the white pith shows, but it will speedily be up again; horse-tails, too, so thick in marshy places—one small species is abundant in the ploughed fields of Surrey, and must be a great trouble to the farmers, for the land is sometimes quite hidden by it.

In the adjoining water tank are the principal flowers and plants which flourish in brook, river, and pond. This yellow iris flowers in many streams about London, and the water-parsnip's pale green foliage waves at the very bottom, for it will grow with the current right over i as well as at the side. Water-plantain grows in every pond near the metropolis; there is some just outside these gardens, in a wet ha-ha.

The huge water-docks in the centre here flourish at the verge of the adjacent Thames; the marsh marigold, now in seed, blooms in April in the damp furrows of meadows close up to town. But in this flower-pot, sunk so as to be in the water, and yet so that the rim may prevent it from spreading and coating the entire tank with green, is the strangest of all, actually duckweed. The still ponds, always found close to cattle yards, are in summer green from end to end with this weed. I recommend all country folk who come up to town in summer time to run down here just to see duckweed cultivated once in their lives.

In front of an ivy-grown museum there is a kind of bowling-green, sunk somewhat below the general surface, where in similar beds may be found the most of those curious old herbs which for seasoning or salad, or some use or superstition, were famous in ancient English households. Not one of them but has its associations. "There's rue for you", to begin with; we all know who that herb is for ever connected with.

There is marjoram and sage, clary, spearmint, peppermint, salsify, elecampane, tansy, assafœtida, coriander, angelica, caper spurge, lamb's lettuce, and sorrel. Mugwort, southernwood, and wormwood are still to be found in old gardens; they stand here side by side. Monkshood, horehound, henbane, vervain (good against the spells of witches), feverfew, dog's mercury, bistort, woad, and so on, all seem like relics of the days of black-letter books. All the while greenfinches are singing happily in the trees without the wall.

Many long summer afternoons would be needed even to glance at all the wild flowers that bloom in June. Then you must come once at least a month, from March to September, as the flowers succeed each other, to read the place aright. It is an index to every meadow and cornfield, wood, heath, and river in the country, and by means of the plants of the same species to the flowers of the world. Therefore, the Herbaceous Ground seems to me a place that should on no account be passed by. And the next place is the Wilderness—that is, the Forest.

On the way thither an old-fashioned yew hedge may be seen round about a vast glasshouse. Outside, on the sward, there are fewer wild flowers growing wild than might perhaps be expected, owing in some degree, no doubt, to the frequent mowing, except under the trees, where again the constant shadow does not suit all. By the ponds, in the midst of trees, and near the river, there is a little grass, however, left to itself, in which in June there were some bird's-foot lotus, veronica, hawkweeds, ox-eye daisy, knapweed, and buttercups. Standing by these ponds, I heard a cuckoo call, and saw a rook sail over them; there was no other sound but that of the birds and the merry laugh of children rolling down the slopes.

The midsummer hum was audible above; the honeydew glistened on the leaves of the limes. There is a sense of repose in the mere aspect of large trees in groups and masses of quiet foliage. Their breadth of form steadies the roving eye; the rounded slopes, the wide sweeping outline of these hills of green boughs, induce an inclination, like them, to rest. To recline upon the grass and with half-closed eyes gaze upon them is enough.

The delicious silence is not the silence of night, of lifelessness; it is the lack of jarring, mechanical noise; it is not silence but the sound of leaf and grass gently stroked by the soft and tender touch of the summer air. It is the sound of happy finches, of the slow buzz of humble-bees, of the occasional splash of a fish, or the call of a moorhen. Invisible in the brilliant beams above, vast legions of insects crowd the sky, but the product of their restless motion is a slumberous hum.

These sounds are the real silence; just as a tiny ripple of the water and the swinging of the shadows as the boughs stoop are the real stillness. If they were absent, if it was the soundlessness and stillness of stone, the mind would crave for something. But these fill and content it. Thus reclining, the storm and stress of life dissolve—there is no thought, no care, no desire. Somewhat of the Nirvana of the earth beneath—the earth which for ever produces and receives back again and yet is for ever at rest—enters into and soothes the heart.

The time slips by, a rook emerges from yonder mass of foliage, and idly floats across, and is hidden in another tree. A whitethroat rises from a bush and nervously discourses, gesticulating with wings and tail, for a few moments. But this is not possible for long; the immense magnetism of London, as I have said before, is too near. There comes the quick short beat of a steam launch shooting down the river hard by, and the dream is over. I rise and go on again.

Already one of the willows planted about the pond is showing the yellow leaf, before midsummer. It reminds me of the inevitable autumn. In October these ponds, now apparently deserted, will be full of moorhens. I have seen and heard but one to-day, but as the autumn comes on they will be here again, feeding about the island, or searching on the sward by the shore. Then, too, among the beeches that lead from hence towards the fanciful pagoda the squirrels will be busy. There are numbers of them, and their motions may be watched with ease. I turn down by the river; in the ditch at the foot of the ha-ha wall is plenty of duckweed, the Lemna of the tank.

A little distance away, and almost on the shore, as it seems, of the Thames, is a really noble horse-chestnut, whose boughs, untouched by cattle, come sweeping down to the ground, and then, continuing, seem to lie on and extend themselves along it, yards beyond their contact. Underneath, it reminds one of sketches of encampments in Hindostan beneath banyan trees, where white tent cloths are stretched from branch to branch. Tent cloths might be stretched here in similar manner, and would enclose a goodly space. Or in the boughs above, a savage's tree hut might be built, and yet scarcely be seen.

My roaming and uncertain steps next bring me under a plane, and I am forced to admire it; I do not like planes, but this is so straight of trunk, so vast of size, and so immense of height that I cannot choose but look up into it. A jackdaw, perched on an upper bough, makes off as I glance up. But the trees constantly afford unexpected pleasure; you wander among the timber of the world, now under the shadow of the trees which the Red Indian haunts, now by those which grow on Himalayan slopes.

The interest lies in the fact that they are trees, not shrubs or mere saplings, but timber trees which cast a broad shadow.

So great is their variety and number that it is not always easy to find an oak or an elm; there are plenty, but they are often lost in the foreign forest. Yet every English shrub and bush is here; the hawthorn, the dogwood, the wayfaring tree, gorse and broom, and here is a round plot of heather. Weary at last, I rest again near the Herbaceous Ground, as the sun declines and the shadows lengthen.

As evening draws on, the whistling of blackbirds and the song of thrushes seem to come from everywhere around. The trees are full of them. Every few moments a blackbird passes over, flying at some height, from the villa gardens and the orchards without. The song increases; the mellow whistling is without intermission; but the shadow has nearly reached the wall, and I must go.

15

The Modern Thames

I

THE WILD RED DEER CAN NEVER AGAIN COME DOWN to drink at the Thames in the dusk of the evening as once they did. While modern civilization endures, the larger fauna must necessarily be confined to parks or restrained to well-marked districts; but for that very reason the lesser creatures of the wood, the field, and the river should receive the more protection. If this applies to the secluded country, far from the stir of cities, still more does it apply to the neighbourhood of London. From a sportsman's point of view, or from that of a naturalist, the state of the river is one of chaos. There is no order. The Thames appears free even from the usual rules which are in force upon every highway. A man may not fire a gun within a certain distance of a road under a penalty—a law enacted for the safety of passengers, who were formerly endangered by persons shooting small birds along the hedges bordering roads. Nor may he shoot at all, not so much as fire off a pistol (as recently publicly proclaimed by the Metropolitan police to restrain the use of revolvers) without a licence. But on the river people do as they choose, and there does not seem to be any law at all—or at least there is no authority to enforce it, if it exists. Shooting from boats and from the towing-path is carried on in utter defiance of the licensing law, of the game law (as applicable to wild fowl), and of the safety of persons who may be passing. The moorhens are shot, the kingfishers have been nearly exterminated or driven away from some parts, the once common black-headed bunting is comparatively scarce in the more frequented reaches, and if there is nothing else to shoot at, then the swallows are slaughtered. Some have even taken to shooting at the rooks in the trees or fields by the river with small-bore rifles—a most dangerous thing to do. The result is that the osier-beds on the eyots and by the backwaters—the copses of the river—are almost devoid of life. A few moorhens creep under the aquatic grasses and conceal themselves beneath the bushes, water-voles hide among the flags, but the once extensive host of water-fowl and river life has been reduced to the smallest limits. Water-fowl cannot breed because they are shot on the nest, or their eggs taken. As for rarer birds, of course they have not the slightest chance.

The fish have fared better because they have received the benefit of close seasons, enforced with more or less vigilance all along the river. They are also protected by regulations making it illegal to capture them except in a sportsmanlike manner; snatching, for instance, is unlawful. Riverside proprietors preserve some reaches, piscatorial societies preserve others, and the complaint indeed is that the rights of the public have been encroached upon. The too exclusive preservation of fish is in a measure responsible for the destruction of water-fowl, which are cleared off preserved places in order that they may not help themselves to fry or spawn. On the other hand, the societies may claim to have saved parts of the river from being entirely deprived of fish, for it is not long since it appeared as if the stream would be quite cleared out. Large quantities of fish have also been placed in the river taken from ponds and bodily transported to the Thames. So that upon the whole the fish have been well looked after of recent years.

The more striking of the aquatic plants—such as white water-lilies—have been much diminished in quantity by the constant plucking, and injury is said to have been done by careless navigation. In things of this kind a few persons can do a great deal of damage. Two or three men with guns, and indifferent to the interests of sport or natural history, at work every day, can clear a long stretch of river of water-fowl, by scaring if not by actually killing them. Imagine three or four such gentry allowed to wander at will in a large game preserve—in a week they would totally destroy it as a preserve. The river, after all, is but a narrow band as it were, and is easily commanded by a gun. So, too, with fish poachers; a very few men with nets can quickly empty a good piece of water: and flowers like water-lilies, which grow only in certain spots, are soon pulled or spoiled. This aspect of the matter—the immense mischief which can be effected by a very few persons—should be carefully borne in mind in framing any regulations. For the mischief done on the river is really the work of a small number, a mere fraction of the thousands of all classes who frequent it. Not one in a thousand probably perpetrates any intentional damage to fish, fowl, or flowers.

As the river above all things is, and ought to be, a place of recreation, care must be particularly taken that in restraining these practices the enjoyment of the many be not interfered with. The rational pleasure of 999 people ought not to be checked because the last of the thousand acts as a blackguard. This point, too, bears upon the question of steam-launches. A launch can pass as softly and quietly as a skiff floating with the stream. And there is a good deal to be said on the other side, for the punts-men stick themselves very often in the way of every one else; and if you analyse fishing for minnows from a punt you will not find it a noble sport. A river like the Thames, belonging as it does—or as it ought—to a city like London, should be managed from the very broadest standpoint. There should be pleasure for all, and there certainly is no real difficulty in arranging matters to that end. The Thames should be like a great aquarium, in which a certain balance of life has to be kept up. When aquaria first came into favour such things as snails and weeds were excluded as eyesores and injurious. But it was soon discovered that the despised snails and weeds were absolutely necessary; an aquarium could not be maintained in health without them, and now the most perfect aquarium is the one in which the natural state is most completely copied. On the same principle it is evident that too exclusive preservation must be injurious to the true interests of the river. Fish enthusiasts, for instance, desire the extinction of water-fowl—there is not a single aquatic bird which they do not accuse of damage to fry, spawn, or full-grown fish; no, not one, from the heron down to the tiny grebe. They are nearly as bitter against animals, the poor water-vole (or water-rat) even is denounced and shot. Any one who chooses may watch the water-rat feeding on aquatic vegetation; never mind, shoot him because he's there. There is no other reason. Bitterest, harshest, most envenomed of all is the outcry and hunt directed against the otter. It is as if the otter were a wolf—as if he were as injurious as the mighty boar whom Meleager and his companions chased in the days of dim antiquity. What, then, has the otter done? Has he ravaged the fields? Does he threaten the homesteads? Is he at Temple Bar? Are we to run, as the old song says, from the Dragon? The fact is, the ravages attributed to the otter are of a local character. They are chiefly committed in those places where fish are more or less confined. If you keep sheep close together in a pen the wolf who leaps the hurdles can kill the flock if he chooses. In narrow waters, and where fish are maintained in quantities out of proportion to extent, an otter can work doleful woe. That is to say, those who want too many fish are those who give the otter his opportunity.

In a great river like the Thames a few otters cannot do much or lasting injury except in particular places. The truth is, that the otter is an ornament to the river, and more worthy of preservation than any other creature. He is the last and largest of the wild creatures who once roamed so freely in the forests which enclosed Londinium, that fort in the woods and marshes—marshes which to this day, though drained and built over, enwrap the nineteenth-century city in thick mists. The red deer are gone, the boar is gone, the wolf necessarily destroyed— the red deer can never again drink at the Thames in the dusk of the evening while our civilization endures. The otter alone remains—the wildest, the most thoroughly self-supporting of all living things left—a living link going back to the days of Cassivelaunus. London ought to take the greatest interest in the otters of its river. The shame-less way in which every otter that dares to show itself is shot, trapped, beaten to death, and literally battered out of existence, should rouse the indignation of every sports-man and every lover of nature. The late Rev. John Russell, who, it will be admitted, was a true sportsman, walked three thousand miles to see an otter. That was a different spirit, was it not?

That is the spirit in which the otter in the Thames should be regarded. Those who offer money rewards for killing Thames otters ought to be looked on as those who would offer rewards for poisoning foxes in Leicestershire. I suppose we shall not see the ospreys again; but I should like to. Again, on the other side of the boundary, in the tidal waters, the same sort of ravenous destruction is carried on against everything that ventures up. A short time ago a porpoise came up to Mortlake; now, just think, a porpoise up from the great sea—that sea to which Londoners rush with such joy—past Gravesend, past Greenwich, past the Tower, under London Bridge, past Westminster and the Houses of Parliament, right up to Mortlake. It is really a wonderful thing that a denizen of the sea, so large and interesting as a porpoise, should come right through the vast City of London. In an aquarium, people would go to see it and admire it, and take their children to see it. What happened? Some one hastened out in a boat, armed with a gun or a rifle, and occupied himself with shooting at it. He did not succeed in killing it, but it was wounded. Some difference here to the spirit of John Russell. If I may be permitted to express an opinion, I think that there is not a single creature, from the sandmarten and the black-headed bunting to the broad-winged heron, from the water-vole to the otter, from the minnow on one side of the tidal boundary to the porpoise on the other—big and little, beasts and birds (of prey or not)—that should not be encouraged and protected on this beautiful river, morally the property of the greatest city in the world.

II

I looked forward to living by the river with delight, anticipating the long rows I should have past the green eyots and the old houses red-tiled among the trees. I should pause below the weir and listen to the pleasant roar, and watch the fisherman cast again and again with the "transcendent patience" of genius by which alone the Thames trout is captured. Twisting the end of a willow

I

bough round my wrist I could moor myself and rest at ease, though the current roared under the skiff, fresh from the waterfall. A thousand thousand bubbles rising to the surface would whiten the stream—a thousand thousand succeeded by another thousand thousand—and still flowing, no multiple could express the endless number. That which flows continuously by some sympathy is acceptable to the mind, as if thereby it realized its own existence without an end. Swallows would skim the water to and fro as yachts tack, the sandpiper would run along the strand, a black-headed bunting would perch upon the willow; perhaps, as the man of genius fishing and myself made no noise, a kingfisher might come, and we might see him take his prey.

Or I might quit hold of the osier, and, entering a shallow backwater, disturb shoals of roach playing where the water was transparent to the bottom, after their wont. Winding in and out like an Indian in his canoe, perhaps traces of an otter might be found—his kitchen mödding— and in the sedges moorhens and wildfowl would hide from me. From its banks I should gather many a flower and notice many a plant, there would be, too, the beautiful water-lily. Or I should row on up the great stream by meadows full of golden buttercups, past fields crimson with trifolium or green with young wheat. Handsome sailing craft would come down spanking before the breeze, laden with bright girls—laughter on board, and love the golden fleece of their argosy.

I should converse with the ancient men of the ferries, and listen to their river lore; they would show me the mark to which the stream rose in the famous year of floods. On again to the cool hostelry whose sign was reflected in the water, where there would be a draught of fine ale for the heated and thirsty sculler. On again till

E.E. BRISCOE.

The SWAN
at Thames Ditton

steeple or tower rising over the trees marked my journey's end for the day, some old town where, after rest and refreshment, there would be a ruin or a timbered house to look at, where I should meet folk full of former days and quaint tales of yore. Thus to journey on from place to place would be the great charm of the river—travelling by water, not merely sculling to and fro, but really travelling. Upon a lake I could but row across and back again, and however lovely the scenery might be, still it would always be the same. But the Thames, upon the river I could really travel, day after day, from Teddington Lock upwards to Windsor, to Oxford, on to quiet Lechlade, or even farther deep into the meadows by Cricklade. Every hour there would be something interesting, all the freshwater life to study, the very barges would amuse me, and at last there would be the delicious ease of floating home carried by the stream, repassing all that had pleased before.

The time came. I lived by the river, not far from its widest reaches, before the stream meets its tide. I went to the eyot for a boat, and my difficulties began. The crowd of boats lashed to each other in strings ready for the hirer disconcerted me. There were so many I could not choose; the whole together looked like a broad raft. Others were hauled on the shore. Over on the eyot, a little island, there were more boats, boats launched, boats being launched, boats being carried by gentlemen in coloured flannels as carefully as mothers handle their youngest infants, boats covered in canvas mummy-cases, and dim boats under roofs, their sharp prows projecting like crocodiles' snouts. Tricksy outriggers, ready to upset on narrow keel, were held firmly for the sculler to step daintily into his place. A strong eight shot by up the stream, the men all pulling together as if they had been one animal. A strong

sculler shot by down the stream, his giant arms bare and
the muscles visible as they rose, knotting and unknotting
with the stroke. Every one on the bank and eyot stopped
to watch him—they knew him, he was training. How
could an amateur venture out and make an exhibition of
himself after such splendid rowing! Still it was noticeable
that plenty of amateurs did venture out, till the waterway
was almost concealed—boated over instead of bridged—
and how they managed to escape locking their oars together,
I could not understand.

I looked again at the boats. Some were outriggers.
I could not get into an outrigger after seeing the great
sculler. The rest were one and all after the same pattern,
i.e., with the stern cushioned and prepared for a lady.
Some were larger, and could carry three or four ladies,
but they were all intended for the same purpose. If the
sculler went out in such a boat by himself he must either
sit too forward and so depress the stem and dig himself,
as it were, into the water at each stroke, or he must sit
too much to the rear and depress the stern, and row with
the stem lifted up, sniffing the air. The whole crowd of
boats on hire were exactly the same; in short, they were
built for woman and not for man, for lovely woman to
recline, parasol in one hand and tiller ropes in the other.
while man—inferior man—pulled and pulled and pulled as
an ox yoked to the plough. They could only be balanced
by man and woman, that was the only way they could be
trimmed on an even keel; they were like scales, in which
the weight on one side must be counterpoised by a weight
in the other. They were dead against bachelors. They
belonged to woman, and she was absolute mistress of the
river.

As I looked, the boats ground together a little, chafing,
laughing at me, making game of me, asking distinctly

what business a man had there without at least one companion in petticoats? My courage ebbed, and it was in
a feeble voice that I inquired whether there was no such
thing as a little skiff a fellow might paddle about in? No,
nothing of the kind; would a canoe do? Somehow a canoe
would not do. I never took kindly to canoes, excepting
always the Canadian birch-bark pattern; evidently there
was no boat for me. There was no place on the great river
for an indolent, dreamy particle like myself, apt to drift
up into nooks, and to spend much time absorbing those
pleasures which enter by the exquisite sensitiveness of the
eye—colour, and shade, and form, and the cadence of
glittering ripple and moving leaf. You must be prepared
to pull and push, and struggle for your existence on the
river, as in the vast city hard by men push and crush for
money. You must assert yourself, and insist upon having
your share of the waterway; you must be perfectly con-
vinced that yours is the very best style of rowing to be
seen; every one ought to get out of your way. You must
consult your own convenience only, and drive right into
other people's boats, forcing them up into the willows,
or against the islands. Never slip along the shore, or into
quiet backwaters; always select the more frequented
parts, not because you want to go there, but to make your
presence known, and go amongst the crowd, and if a few
sculls get broken, it only proves how very inferior and
how very clumsy other people are.

If you see another boat coming down stream in the
centre of the river with a broad space on either side for
others to pass, at once head your own boat straight at her,
and take possession of the way. Or, better still, never look
ahead, but pull straight on, and let things happen as they
may. Annoy everybody, and you are sure to be right, and
to be respected; splash the ladies as you pass with a dex-

terous flip of the scull, and soak their summer costumes; it is capital sport and they look so sulky—or is it contemptuous?

There was no such thing as a skiff in which one could quietly paddle about, or gently make way—mile after mile—up the beautiful stream. The boating throng grew thicker, and my courage less and less, till I desperately resorted to the ferry-boat, that would be something; I should be on the water, after a fashion—and the ferry-man would know a good deal. The burly ferryman said nothing or "No"; he was full of the Derby and Sandown; didn't know about the fishing; supposed there were fish; didn't see 'em, nor eat 'em; want a punt? No. So he landed me, desolate and hopeless, on the opposite bank, and I began to understand how the souls felt after Charon had got them over. They would not have been more unhappy than I was on the towing-path as the ferry-boat receded and left me watching the continuous succession of boats passing up and down the river.

By-and-by an immense black hulk came drifting round the bend—an empty barge—almost broadside across the stream, for the current at the curve naturally carried it out from the shore. This huge helpless monster occupied the whole river, and had no idea where it was going, for it had no fins or sweeps to guide its course, and the rudder could only induce it to submit itself lengthways to the stream after the lapse of some time. The fairway of the river was entirely taken up by this irresponsible Frankenstein of the Thames, which some one had started, but which now did as it liked. Some of the small craft got up into the willows and waited; some seemed narrowly to escape being crushed against a wall on the opposite bank. The bright white sails of a yacht shook and quivered as its steersman tried all he knew to coax his vessel an inch more into the wind out of the monster's path. In vain!

He had to drop down the stream, and lose what it had taken him half an hour's skill to gain. What a pleasing monster to meet in the narrow arches of a bridge! The man in charge leaned on the tiller and placidly gazed at the wild efforts of some unskilful oarsmen to escape collision. In fact, the monster had charge of the man, and did as it liked with him.

Down the river they drifted together, Frankenstein swinging round and thrusting his blunt nose first this way and then that; down the river, blocking up the narrow passage by the eyot; stopping the traffic at the lock; out at last into the tidal stream, there to begin a fresh life of annoyance, and finally to endanger the good speed of many a fine three-master and ocean steamer off the docks. The Thames barge knows no law. No judge, no jury, no Palace of Justice, no Chancery, no appeal to the Lords has any terror for the monster barge. It drifts by the Houses of Parliament with no more respect than it shows for the lodge of the lock-keeper. It drifts by Royal Windsor and cares not. The guns of the Tower are of no account. There is nothing in the world so utterly free as this monster.

Often have I asked myself if the bargee at the tiller, now sucking at his short black pipe, now munching onions and cheese (the little onions he pitches on the lawns by the river side, there to take root and flourish)—if this amiable man has any notion of his own incomparable position. Just some inkling of the irony of the situation must, I fancy, now and then dimly dawn within his grimy brow. To see all these gentlemen shoved on one side; to be lying in the way of a splendid Australian clipper; to stop an incoming vessel, impatient for her berth; to swing, and sway, and roll as he goes; to bump the big ships, and force the little ones aside; to slip, and slide, and glide with the tide, ripples dancing under the prow, and be master of the world-famed Thames from source to mouth, is not this a joy for ever? Liberty is beyond price; now no one is really free unless he can crush his neighbour's interest underfoot, like a horse-roller going over a daisy. Bargee is free, and the ashes of his pipe are worth a king's ransom. Imagine a great van loaded at the East-end of London with the heaviest merchandise, with bags of iron nails, shot, leaden sheets in rolls, and pig iron; imagine four strong horses—dray-horses—harnessed thereto. Then let the waggoner mount behind in a seat comfortably contrived for him facing the rear, and settle himself down happily among his sacks, light his pipe, and fold his hands untroubled with any worry of reins. Away they go through the crowded city, by the Bank of England, and across into Cheapside, cabs darting this way, carriages that, omnibuses forced up into side-streets, foot traffic suspended till the monster has passed; up Fleet Street, clearing the road in front of them—right through the stream of lawyers always rushing to and fro the Temple and the New Law Courts, along the Strand, and finally in triumph into Rotten Row at five o'clock on a June afternoon. See how they scatter! see how they run! The Row is swept clear from end to end—beauty, fashion, rank,—what are such trifles of an hour? The monster vans grind them all to powder. What such a waggoner might do on land, bargee does on the river.

Of olden times the silver Thames was the chosen mode of travel of Royalty—the highest in the land were rowed from palace to city, or city to palace, between its sunlit banks. Noblemen had their special oarsmen, and were in like manner conveyed, and could any other mode of journeying be equally pleasant? The coal-barge has bumped them all out of the way.

No man dares send forth the commonest cart unless in proper charge, and if the horse is not under control a fine is promptly administered. The coal-barge rolls and turns and drifts as chance and the varying current please. How huge must be the rent in the meshes of the law to let so large a fish go through! But in truth there is no law about it, and to this day no man can confidently affirm that he knows to whom the river belongs. These curious anomalies are part and parcel of our political system, and as I watched the black monster slowly go by with the stream it occurred to me that grimy bargee, with his short pipe and his onions, was really the guardian of the British Constitution.

Hardly had he gone past than a loud pant! pant! pant! began some way down the river; it came from a tug, whose short puffs of steam produced a giant echo against the walls and quays and houses on the bank. These angry pants sounded high above the splash of oars and laughter, and the chorus of singers in a boat; they conquered all other sounds and noises, and domineered the place. It was impossible to shut the ears to them, or to persuade the mind not to heed. The swallows dipped their breasts; how gracefully they drank on the wing! Pant! pant! pant! The sunlight gleamed on the wake of a four-oar. Pant! pant! pant! The soft wind blew among the trees and over the hawthorn hedge. Pant! pant! pant! Neither the eye nor ear could attend to aught but this hideous uproar. The tug was weak, the stream strong, the barges behind heavy, broad, and deeply laden, so that each puff and pant and turn of the screw barely advanced the mass a foot. There are many feet in a mile, and for all that weary time— Pant! pant! pant! This dreadful uproar, like that which Don Quixote and Sancho Panza heard proceeding from the fulling mill, must be endured. Could not philosophy by stoic firmness shut out the sound? Can philosophy shut out anything that is real? A long black streak of smoke hung over the water, fouling the gleaming surface. A noise of Dante—hideous, uncompromising as the rusty hinge of the gate which forbids hope. Pant! pant! pant!

Once upon a time a Queen of England was rowed down the silver Thames to the sweet low sound of the flute. At last the noise grew fainter in the distance, and the black hulls disappeared round the bend. I walked on up the towing-path.

Accidentally lifting my hand to shade my eyes, I was hailed by a ferry-man on the watch. He conveyed me over without much volition, and set me ashore by the inn of my imagination. The rooms almost overhung the water; so far my vision was fulfilled. Within there was an odour of spirits and spilled ale, a rustle of sporting papers, talk of racings, and the click of billiard-balls. Without there were two or three loafers, half-boatmen, half-vagabonds, waiting to pick up stray sixpences—a sort of leprosy of rascal and sneak in their faces and the lounge of their bodies.

These Thames-side "beach-combers" are a sorry lot, a special Pariah class of themselves. Some of them have been men once; perhaps one retains his sculling skill, and is occasionally engaged by a gentleman to give him lessons. They regarded me eagerly—they "spotted" a Thames freshman who might be made to yield silver; but I walked away down the road into the village.

The spire of the church interested me, being of shingles —i.e. of wooden slates—as the houses are roofed in America, as houses were roofed in Elizabethan England; for young America reproduces Old England even in roofs. Some of the houses so closely approached the churchyard that the pantry windows on a level with the ground were

partly blocked up by the green mounds of graves. Borage
grew thickly all over the yard, dropping its blue flowers
on the dead. The sharp note of a bugle rang in the air:
they were changing the guard, I suppose, in Wolsey's
Palace.

III

In time I did discover a skiff moored in a little-visited
creek, which the boatman got out for me. The sculls were
rough and shapeless—it is a remarkable fact that sculls
always are, unless you have them made and keep them for
your own use. I paddled up the river; I paused by an osier-
grown islet; I slipped past the barges, and avoided an
unskilful party; it was the morning, and none of the up-
roarious as yet were about. Certainly, it was very pleasant.
The sunshine gleamed on the water, broad shadows of
trees fell across; swans floated in the by-channels. A peace-
fulness which peculiarly belongs to water hovered above
the river. A house-boat was moored near the willow-
grown shore, and it was evidently inhabited, for there
was a fire smouldering on the bank, and some linen that
had been washed spread on the bushes to bleach. All the
windows of this gipsy-van of the river were wide open,
and the air and light entered freely into every part of the
dwelling-house under which flowed the stream. A lady
was dressing herself before one of these open windows,
twining up large braids of dark hair, her large arms bare
to the shoulder, and somewhat farther. I immediately
steered out into the channel to avoid intrusion; but I felt
that she was regarding me with all a matron's contempt
for an unknown man—a mere member of the opposite
sex, not introduced, or of her "set". I was merely a man—
no more than a horse on the bank,—and had she been in
her smock she would have been just as indifferent.

Certainly it was a lovely morning; the old red palace of the Cardinal seemed to slumber amid its trees, as if the passage of the centuries had stroked and soothed it into indolent peace. The meadows rested; even the swallows, the restless swallows, glided in an effortless way through the busy air. I could see this, and yet I did not quite enjoy it; something drew me away from perfect contentment, and gradually it dawned upon me that it was the current causing an unsuspected amount of labour in sculling. The forceless particles of water, so yielding to the touch, which slipped aside at the motion of the oar, in their countless myriads, ceaselessly flowing grew to be almost a solid obstruction to the boat. I had not noticed it for a mile or so; now the pressure of the stream was becoming evident. I persuaded myself that it was nothing. I held on by the boathook to a root and rested, and so went on again. Another mile or more; another rest: decidedly sculling against a swift current is work—downright work. You have no energy to spare over and above that needed for the labour of rowing, not enough even to look round and admire the green loveliness of the shore. I began to think that I should not get as far as Oxford after all.

By-and-by, I began to question if rowing on a river is as pleasant as rowing on a lake, where you can rest on your oars without losing ground, where no current opposes progress, and after the stroke the boat slips ahead some distance of its own impetus. On the river the boat only travels as far as you actually pull it at each stroke; there is no life in it after the scull is lifted, the impetus dies, and the craft first pauses and then drifts backwards. I crept along the shore, so near that one scull occasionally grounded, to avoid the main force of the water, which is in the middle of the river. I slipped behind eyots and tried all I knew. In vain, the river was stronger than I, and my arms could not for many hours contend with the Thames. So faded another part of my dream. The idea of rowing from one town to another—of expeditions and travelling across the country, so pleasant to think of—in practice became impossible. An athlete bent on nothing but athleticism—a canoeist thinking of nothing but his canoe —could accomplish it, setting himself daily so much work to do, and resolutely performing it. A dreamer, who wanted to enjoy his passing moment, and not to keep regular time with his strokes, who wanted to gather flowers, and indulge his luxurious eyes with effects of light and shadow and colour, could not succeed. The river is for the man of might.

With a weary back at last I gave up the struggle at the foot of a weir, almost in the splash of the cascade. My best friend, the boathook, kept me stationary without effort, and in time rest restored the strained muscles to physical equanimity. The roar of the river falling over the dam soothed the mind—the sense of an immense power at hand, working with all its might while you are at ease, has a strangely soothing influence. It makes me sleepy to see the vast beam of an engine regularly rise and fall in ponderous irresistible labour. Now at last some fragment of my fancy was realized—a myriad myriad rushing bubbles whitening the stream burst, and were instantly succeeded by myriads more; the boat faintly vibrated as the wild waters shot beneath it; the green cascade, smooth at its first curve, dashed itself into the depth beneath, broken to a million million particles; the eddies whirled, and sucked, and sent tiny whirlpools rotating along the surface; the roar rose or lessened in intensity as the velocity of the wind varied; sunlight sparkled—the warmth inclined the senses to a drowsy idleness. Yonder was the trout fishermen, just as I had imagined him, casting and casting again with that transcendental patience which is genius; his line and the top of his rod formed momentary curves pleasant to look at. The kingfisher did not come—no doubt he had been shot—but a reed-sparrow did, in velvet black cap and dainty brown, pottering about the willow near me. This was really like the beautiful river I had dreamed of. If only we could persuade ourselves to remain quiescent when we are happy! If only we would remain still in the armchair as the last curl of vapour rises from a cigar that has been enjoyed! If only we would sit still in the shadow and not go indoors to write that letter! Let happiness alone. Stir not an inch; speak not a word: happiness is a coy maiden—hold her hand and be still.

In an evil moment I spied the corner of a newspaper projecting from the pocket of my coat in the stern-sheets. Folly led me to open that newspaper, and in it I saw and read a ghastly paragraph. Two ladies and a gentleman while boating had been carried by the current against the piles of a weir. The boat upset; the ladies were rescued, but the unfortunate gentleman was borne over the fall and drowned. His body had not been recovered; men were watching the pool day and night till some chance eddy should bring it to the surface. So perished my dream, and the coy-maiden happiness left me because I could not be content to be silent and still. The accident had not happened at this weir, but it made no difference; I could see all as plainly. A white face, blurred and indistinct, seemed to rise up from beneath the rushing bubbles till, just as it was about to jump to the surface, as things do that come up, down it was drawn again by that terrible underpull which has been fatal to so many good swimmers.

Who can keep afloat with a force underneath dragging at the feet? Who can swim when the water—all bubbles, that is air—gives no resistance to the hands? Hands and feet slip through the bubbles. You might as well spring from the parapet of a house and think to float by striking out as to swim in such a medium. Sinking under, a hundred tons of water drive the body to the bottom; there it rotates, it rises, it is forced down again, a hundred tons of water beat upon it; the foot, perhaps, catches among stones or woodwork, and what was once a living being is imprisoned in death. Enough of this. I unloosed the boathook, and drifted down with the stream, anxious to get away from the horrible weir.

These accidents, which are entirely preventable, happen year after year with lamentable monotony. Each weir is a little Niagara, and a boat once within its influence is certain to be driven to destruction. The current carries it against the piles, where it is either broken or upset, the natural and reasonable alarm of the occupants increasing the risk. In descending the river every boat must approach the weir, and must pass within a few yards of the dangerous current. If there is a press of boats one is often forced out of the proper course into the rapid part of the stream without any negligence on the part of those in it. There is nothing to prevent this—no fence, or boom; no mark, even, between what is dangerous and what is not; no division whatever. Persons ignorant of the river may just as likely as not row right into danger. A vague caution on a notice-board may or may not be seen; in either case it gives no directions, and is certainly no protection. Let the matter be argued from whatever point of view, the fact remains that these accidents occur from the want of an efficient division between the dangerous and the safe part of the approach to a weir. A boom or some kind of fence is required, and how extraordinary it seems that nothing of the kind is done! It is not done because there is no authority, no control, no one responsible. Two or three gentlemen acquainted with aquatics could manage the river from end to end, to the safety and satisfaction of all, if they were entrusted with discretionary powers. Stiff rules and rigid control are not needed; what is wanted is a rational power freely using its discretion. I do not mean a Board with its attendant follies; I mean a small committee, unfettered, untrammelled by "legal advisers" and so forth, merely using their own good sense.

I drifted away from the weir—now grown hideous—and out of hearing of its wailing dirge for the unfortunate. I drifted past more barges coming up, and more steam-tugs; past river lawns, where gay parties were now sipping claret-cup or playing tennis. By-and-by, I began to meet pleasure-boats and to admire their manner of progress. First there came a gentleman in white flannels, walking on the towpath, with a rope round his waist, towing a boat in which two ladies were comfortably seated. In a while came two more gentlemen in striped flannels, one streaked with gold the other with scarlet, striding side by side and towing a boat in which sat one lady. They were very earnestly at work, pacing in step, their bodies slightly leaning forwards, and every now and then they mopped their faces with handkerchiefs which they carried in their girdles. Something in their slightly-bowed attitude reminded me of the captives depicted on Egyptian monuments, with cords about their necks. How curious is that instinct which makes each sex, in different ways, the willing slave of the other! These human steam-tugs paced and pulled, and drew the varnished craft swiftly against the stream, evidently determined to do a certain distance by a certain hour. As I drifted by without labour, I admired them very much. An interval, and still more gentlemen in flannel, labouring like galley-slaves at the tow-rope, hot, perspiring, and happy after their kind, and ladies under parasols, comfortably seated, cool, and happy after their kind.

Considering upon these things, I began to discern the true and only manner in which the modern Thames is to be enjoyed. Above all things—nothing heroic. Don't scull—don't row—don't haul at tow-ropes—don't swim—don't flourish a fishing-rod. Set your mind at ease. Make friends with two or more athletes, thorough good fellows, good-natured, delighting in their thews and sinews. Explain to them that somehow, don't you see, nature did not bless you with such superabundant muscularity, although there is nothing under the sun you admire so much. Forthwith these good fellows will pet you, and your Thames fortune is made. You take your place in the stern-sheets, happily protected on either side by feminine human nature, and the parasols meeting above shield you from the sun. The tow-rope is adjusted, and the tugs start. The gliding motion soothes the soul. Feminine boating nature has no antipathy to the cigarette. A delicious odour, soft as new-mown hay, a hint of spices and distant flowers—sunshine dried and preserved, sunshine you can handle—rises from the smouldering fibres. This is smoking summer itself. Yonder in the fore part of the craft I espy certain vessels of glass on which is the label of Epernay. And of such is peace.

Drifting ever downwards, I approached the creek where my skiff had to be left; but before I reached it a "beach-comber", with a coil of cord over his shoulder, asked me if he should tow me "up to 'Ampton". I shook my head, whereupon he abused me in such choice terms that I listened abashed at my ignorance. It had never occurred to me that swearing could be done like that. It is true we have been swearing now, generation after generation, these eight thousand years for certain, and language ex-

K

pands with use. It is also true that we are all educated now. Shakespeare is credited with knowing everything, past or future, but I doubt if he knew how a Thames "beach-comber" can curse in these days.

The Thames is swearing free. You must moderate your curses on the Queen's highway; you must not be even profane in the streets, lest you be taken before the magistrates; but on the Thames you may swear as the wind blows—howsoever you list. You may begin at the mouth, off the Nore, and curse your way up to Cricklade. A hundred miles for swearing is a fine preserve. It is one of the marvels of our civilization.

Aided by scarce a touch of the sculls the stream drifted me up into the creek, and the boatman took charge of his skiff. "Shall I keep her handy for you, sir?" he said, thinking to get me down every day as a newcomer. I begged him not to put himself to any trouble, still he repeated that he would keep her ready. But in the road I shook off the dust of my feet against the river, and earnestly resolved never, never again to have anything to do with it (in the heroic way) lower down than Henley.

16

On the London Road

THE ROAD COMES STRAIGHT FROM LONDON, WHICH IS but a very short distance off, within a walk, yet the village it passes is thoroughly a village, and not suburban, not in the least like Sydenham, or Croydon, or Balham, or Norwood, as perfect a village in every sense as if it stood fifty miles in the country. There is one long street, just as would be found in the far west, with fields at each end. But through this long street, and on and out into the open, is continually pouring the human living undergrowth of that vast forest of life, London. The nondescript inhabitants of the thousand and one nameless streets of the unknown east are great travellers, and come forth into the country by this main desert route. For what end? Why this tramping and ceaseless movement? What do they buy, what do they sell, how do they live? They pass through the village street and out into the country in an endless stream on the shutter on wheels. This is the true London vehicle, the characteristic conveyance, as characteristic as the Russian droshky, the gondola at Venice, or the caique at Stamboul. It is the camel of the London desert routes; routes which run right through civilization, but of which daily paper civilization is ignorant. People who can pay for a daily paper are so far above it; a daily paper is the mark of the man who is in civilization.

Take an old-fashioned shutter and balance it on the axle of a pair of low wheels, and you have the London camel in principle. To complete it add shafts in front, and at the rear run a low free-board, as a sailor would say, along the edge, that the cargo may not be shaken off. All the skill of the fashionable brougham-builders in Long Acre could not contrive a vehicle which would meet the requirements of the case so well as this. On the desert routes of Palestine a donkey becomes romantic; in a costermonger's barrow he is only an ass; the donkey himself doesn't see the distinction. He draws a good deal of human nature about in these barrows, and perhaps finds it very much the same in Surrey and Syria. For if any one thinks the familiar barrow is merely a truck for the conveyance of cabbages and carrots, and for the exposure of the same to the choice of housewives in Bermondsey, he is mistaken. Far beyond that, it is the symbol, the solid expression, of life itself to the owner, his family, and circle of connections, more so than even the ship to the sailor, as the sailor, no matter how he may love his ship, longs for port, and the joys of the shore, but the barrow folk are always at sea on land. Such care has to be taken of the miserable pony or the shamefaced jackass; he has to be groomed, and fed, and looked to in his shed, and this occupies three or four of the family at least, lads and strapping young girls, night and morning. Besides which, the circle of connections look in to see how he is going on, and to hear the story of the day's adventures, and what is proposed for to-morrow. Perhaps one is invited to join the next excursion, and thinks as much of it as others might do of an invitation for a cruise in the Mediterranean. Any one who watches the succession of barrows driving along through the village out into the fields of Kent can easily see how they bear upon their wheels the fortunes of whole families and of their hangers-on. Sometimes there is a load of pathos, of which the race of the ass has carried a good deal in all

Cloth Fair, Smithfield.

E. E. BRISCOE

ages. More often it is a heavy lump of dull, evil, and exceedingly stupid cunning. The wild evil of the Spanish contrabandists seems atoned by that wildness; but this dull wickedness has no flush of colour, no poppy on its dirt heaps.

Over one barrow the sailors had fixed up a tent— canvas stretched from corner poles, two fellows sat almost on the shafts outside; they were well. Under the canvas there lay a young fellow white and emaciated, whose face was drawn down with severe suffering of some kind, and his dark eyes, enlarged and accentuated, looked as if touched with belladonna. The family council at home in the close and fetid court had resolved themselves into a medical board and ordered him to the sunny Riviera. The ship having been fitted up for the invalid, away they sailed for the south, out from the ends of the earth of London into the ocean of green fields and trees, thence past many an island village, and so to the shores where the Kentish hops were yellowing fast for the pickers. There, in the vintage days, doubtless he found solace, and possibly recovery. To catch a glimpse of that dark and cavernous eye under the shade of the travelling tent reminded me of the eyes of the wounded in the ambulance-waggons that came pouring into Brussels after Sedan. In the dusk of the lovely September evenings—it was a beautiful September, the lime-leaves were just tinted with orange— the waggons came in a long string, the wounded and maimed lying in them, packed carefully, and rolled round, as it were, with wadding to save them from the jolts of the ruts and stones. It is fifteen years ago, and yet I can still distinctly see the eyes of one soldier looking at me from his berth in the waggon. The glow of intense pain—the glow of long-continued agony—lit them up as coals that smouldering are suddenly fanned. Pain brightens the eyes as much as joy, there is a fire in the brain behind it; it is the flame in the mind you see, and not the eyeball. A thought that might easily be rendered romantic, but consider how these poor fellows appeared afterwards. Bevies of them hopped about Brussels in their red-and-blue uniforms, some on crutches, some with two sticks, some with sleeves pinned to their breasts, looking exactly like a company of dolls a cruel child had mutilated, snapping a foot off here, tearing out a leg here, and battering the face of a third. Little men most of them—the bowl of a German pipe inverted would have covered them all, within which, like bees in a hive, they might hum "Te Deum Bismarckum Laudamus." But the romantic flame in the eye is not always so beautiful to feel as to read about.

Another shutter on wheels went by one day with one little pony in the shafts, and a second harnessed in some way at the side, so as to assist in pulling, but without bearing any share of the load. On this shutter eight men and boys balanced themselves; enough for the Olympian height of a four-in-hand. Eight fellows perched round the edge like shipwrecked mariners, clinging to one plank. They were so balanced as to weight chiefly on the axle, yet in front of such a mountain of men, such a vast bundle of ragged clothes, the ponies appeared like rats.

On a Sunday morning two fellows came along on their shutter: they overtook a girl who was walking on the pavement, and one of them, more sallow and cheeky than his companion, began to talk to her. "That's a nice nosegay, now—give us a rose. Come and ride—there's plenty of room. Won't speak? Now, you'll tell us if this is the road to London Bridge." She nodded. She was dressed in full satin for Sunday; her class think much of satin. She was leading two children, one in each hand, clean and well-dressed. She walked more lightly than

a servant does, and evidently lived at home; she did not
go to service. Tossing her head, she looked the other
way, for you see the fellow on the shutter was dirty, not
"dressed" at all, though it was Sunday, poor folks' ball-
day; a dirty, rough fellow, with a short clay pipe in his
mouth, a chalky-white face—apparently from low dis-
sipation—a disreputable rascal, a monstrously impudent
"chap", a true London mongrel. He "cheeked" her; she
tossed her head, and looked the other way. But by-and-by
she could not help a sly glance at him, not an angry
glance—a look as much as to say, "You're a man, anyway,
and you've the good taste to admire me, and the courage
to speak to me; you're dirty, but you're a man. If you were
well-dressed, or if it wasn't Sunday, or if it was dark, or
nobody about, I wouldn't mind; I'd let you 'cheek' me,
though I have got satin on." The fellow "cheeked" her
again, told her she had a pretty face, "cheeked" her right
and left. She looked away, but half-smiled; she had to
keep up her dignity, she did not feel it. She would have
liked to have joined company with him. His leer grew
leerier—the low, cunning leer, so peculiar to the London
mongrel, that seems to say, "I am so intensely knowing;
I am so very much all there"; and yet the leerer always
remains in a dirty dress, always smokes the coarsest
tobacco in the nastiest of pipes, and rides on a barrow to
the end of his life. For his leery cunning is so intensely
stupid that, in fact, he is as "green" as grass; his leer and
his foul mouth keep him in the gutter to his very last day.
How much more successful plain, simple straightforward-
ness would be! The pony went on a little, but they drew
rein and waited for the girl again; and again he "cheeked"
her. Still, she looked away, but she did not make any
attempt to escape by the side-path, nor show resentment.
No; her face began to glow, and once or twice she answered

him, but still she would not quite join company. If only it had not been Sunday—if it had been a lonely road, and not so near the village, if she had not had the two tell-tale children with her—she would have been very good friends with the dirty, chalky, ill-favoured, and ill-savoured wretch. At the parting of the roads each went different ways, but she could not help looking back.

He was a thorough specimen of the leery London mongrel. That hideous leer is so repulsive—one cannot endure it—but it is so common; you see it on the faces of four-fifths of the ceaseless stream that runs out from the ends of the earth of London into the green sea of the country. It disfigures the faces of the carters who go with the waggons and other vehicles—not nomads, but men in steady employ; it defaces—absolutely defaces—the workmen who go forth with vans, with timber, with carpenters' work, and the policemen standing at the corners, in London itself particularly. The London leer hangs on their faces. The Mosaic account of the Creation is discredited in these days, the last revelation took place at Beckenham; the Beckenham revelation is superior to Mount Sinai, yet the consideration of that leer might suggest the idea of a fall of man even to an Amœbist. The horribleness of it is in this way, it hints—it does more than hint, it conveys the leerer's decided opinion—that you, whether you may be man or woman, must necessarily be as coarse as himself. Especially he wants to impress that view upon every woman who chances to cross his glance. The fist of Hercules is needed to dash it out of his face.

17

Venice in the East End

THE GREAT RED BOWSPRIT OF AN AUSTRALIAN clipper projects aslant the quay. Stem to the shore, the vessel thrusts an outstretched arm high over the land, as an oak in a glade pushes a bare branch athwart the opening. This beam is larger than an entire tree divested of its foliage, such trees, that is, as are seen in English woods. The great oaks might be bigger at the base where they swell and rest themselves on a secure pedestal. Five hundred years old an oak might measure more at six feet, at eight, or ten feet from the ground; after five hundred years, that is, of steady growth. But if even such a monarch were taken, and by some enormous mechanic power drawn out, and its substance elongated into a tapering spar, it would not be massive enough to form this single beam. Where it starts from the stem of the vessel it is already placed as high above the level of the quay as it is from the sward to the first branch of an oak. At its root it starts high overhead, high enough for a trapeze to be slung to it upon which grown persons could practise athletic exercises. From its roots, from the forward end of the deck, the red beam rises at a regular angle, diminishing in size with altitude till its end in comparison with the commencement may be called pointed, though in reality blunt. To the pointed end it would be a long climb; it would need a ladder. The dull red of the vast beam is obscured by the neutral tint of the ropes which are attached to it; colour generally gives a sense of lightness by defining shape, but this red is worn and weatherbeaten, rubbed and battered, so that its uncertain surface adds to the weight of the boom.

It hangs, an immense arm thrust across the sky; it is so high it is scarcely noticed in walking under it; it is so great and ponderous, and ultra in size, that the eye and mind alike fail to estimate it. For it is a common effect of great things to be overlooked. A moderately large rock, a moderately large house, is understood and mentally put down, as it were, at a certain figure, but the immense—which is beyond the human—cannot enter the organs of the senses. The portals of the senses are not wide enough to receive it; you must turn your back on it and reflect, and add a little piece of it to another little piece, and so build up your understanding. Human things are small; you live in a large house, but the space you actually occupy is very inconsiderable; the earth itself, great as it is, is overlooked, it is too large to be seen. The eye is accustomed to the little, and cannot in a moment receive the immense. Only by slow comparison with the bulk of oak trees, by the height of a trapeze, by the climbing of a ladder, can I convey to my mind a true estimate and idea of this gigantic bowsprit. It would be quite possible to walk by and never see it because of its size, as one walks by bridges or travels over a viaduct without a thought.

The vessel lies with her bowsprit projecting over the quay, moored as a boat run ashore on the quiet sandy beach of a lake, not as a ship is generally placed with her broadside to the quay wall or to the pier. Her stern is yonder—far out in the waters of the dock, too far to concern us much as we look from the verge of the wall. Access to the ship is obtained by a wooden staging running out at the side; instead of the ship lying beside the pier, a pier has been built out to fit to the ship. This plan, contrary to preconceived ideas, is evidently founded on

good reason, for if such a vessel were moored broadside
to the quay how much space would she take up? There
would be, first, the hull itself, say eighty yards, and then
the immense bowsprit. Two or three such ships would,
as it were, fill a whole field of water; they would fill
a whole dock; it would not require many to cover a mile.
By placing each stem to the quay they only occupy a space
equal to their breadth instead of to their length. This
arrangement, again, tends to deceive the eye; you might
pass by, and, seeing only the bow, casually think there
was nothing particular in it. Everything here is on so
grand a scale that the largest component part is diminished;
the quay, broad enough to build several streets abreast;
the square, open stretches of gloomy water; and beyond
these the wide river. The wind blows across these open
spaces in a broad way—not as it comes in sudden gusts
around a street corner, but in a broad open way, each puff
a quarter of a mile wide. The view of the sky is open
overhead, masts do not obstruct the upward look; the
sunshine illumines or the cloud-shadows darken hundreds
of acres at once. It is a great plain; a plain of enclosed
waters, built in and restrained by the labour of man, and
holding upon its surface fleet upon fleet, argosy upon
argosy. Masts to the right, masts to the left, masts in front,
masts yonder above the warehouses; masts in among the
streets as steeples appear amid roofs; masts across the river
hung with drooping half-furled sails; masts afar down thin
and attenuated, mere dark straight lines in the distance.
They await in stillness the rising of the tide.

It comes, and at the exact moment—foreknown to
a second—the gates are opened, and the world of ships
moves outwards to the stream. Downwards they drift to
the east, some slowly that have as yet but barely felt the
pull of the hawser, others swiftly, and the swifter because

their masts cross and pass the masts of inward-bound
ships ascending. Two lines of masts, one raking one way,
the other the other, cross and puzzle the eye to separate
their weaving motion and to assign the rigging to the
right vessel. White funnels aslant, dark funnels, red funnels
rush between them; white steam curls upwards; there is
a hum, a haste, almost a whirl, for the commerce of the
world is crowded into the hour of the full tide. These
great hulls, these crossing masts a-rake, the intertangled
rigging, the background of black barges drifting downwards, the lines and ripple of the water as the sun comes
out, if you look too steadily, daze the eyes and cause a sense
of giddiness. It is so difficult to realize so much mass—
so much bulk—moving so swiftly, and in so intertangled
a manner; a mighty dance of thousands of tons—gliding,
slipping, drifting onwards, yet without apparent effort.
Thousands upon thousands of tons go by like shadows,
silently, as if the ponderous hulls had no stability or
weight; like a dream they float past, solid and yet without
reality. It is a giddiness to watch them.

This happens, not on one day only, not one tide, but at
every tide and every day the year through, year after year.
The bright summer sun glows upon it; the red sun of the
frosty hours of winter looks at it from under the deepen-
ing canopy of vapour; the blasts of the autumnal equinox
howl over the vast city and whistle shrilly in the rigging;
still at every tide the world of ships moves out into the
river. Why does not a painter come here and place the
real romance of these things upon canvas, as Venice has
been placed? Never twice alike, the changing atmosphere
is reflected in the hue of the varnished masts, now gleaming, now dull, now dark. Till it has been painted, and sung
by poet, and described by writers, nothing is human.
Venice has been made human by poet, painter, and

dramatiſt, yet what was Venice to this—this the Faɛt of our own day? Two of the caravels of the Doge's fleet, two of Othello's ſtrongeſt war-ships, could scarcely carry the maſt of my Auſtralian clipper. At a guess it is four feet through; it is of iron, tubular; there is room for a winding spiral ſtaircase within it; as for its height, I will not risk a guess at it. Could Othello's war-ships carry it they would consider it a feat, as the bringing of the Egyptian obelisk to London was thought a feat. The petty ripples of the Adriatic, what were they? This red bowsprit at its roots is high enough to suspend a trapeze; at its head a ladder would be required to mount it from the quay; yet by-and-by, when the tide at laſt comes, and its time arrives to move outwards in the dance of a million tons, this mighty bowsprit, meeting the Atlantic rollers in the Bay of Biscay, will dip and bury itself in foam under the ſtress of the vaſt sails aloft. The forty-feet billows of the Pacific will swing these three or four thousand or more tons, this giant hull which muſt be moored even ſtem to shore, up and down and side to side as a handful in the grasp of the sea. Now, each night as the clouds part, the north ſtar looks down upon the deck; then, the Southern Cross will be visible in the sky, words quickly written, but half a globe apart. What was there in Venice to arouse thoughts such as spring from the sight of this red bowsprit? In two voyages my Auſtralian clipper shall carry as much merchandise as shall equal the entire commerce of Venice for a year.

Yet it is not the volume, not the bulk only; cannot you see the white sails swelling, and the proud vessel rising to the Pacific billows, the north ſtar sinking, and the advent of the Southern Cross; the thousand miles of ocean without land around, the voyage through space made visible as sea, the far, far south, the transit around a world?

If Italian painters had had such things as these to paint, if poets of old time had had such things as these to sing, do you imagine they would have been contented with crank caravels and tales thrice told already? They had eyes to see that which was around them. Open your eyes and see those things which are around us at this hour.

18

Red Roofs of London

TILES AND TILE ROOFS HAVE A CURIOUS WAY OF tumbling to pieces in an irregular and eye-pleasing manner. The roof-tree bends, bows a little under the weight, curves in, and yet preserves a sharpness at each end. The Chinese exaggerate this curve of set purpose. Our English curve is softer, being the product of time, which always works in true taste. The mystery of tile-laying is not known to every one; for to all appearance tiles seem to be put on over a thin bed of hay or hay-like stuff. Lately they have begun to use some sort of tarpaulin or a coarse material of that kind; but the old tiles, I fancy, were comfortably placed on a shake-down of hay. When one slips off, little bits of hay stick up; and to these the sparrows come, removing it bit by bit to line their nests. If they can find a gap they get in, and a fresh couple is started in life. By-and-by a chimney is overthrown during a twist of the wind, and half a dozen tiles are shattered. Time passes; and at last the tiler arrives to mend the mischief. His labour leaves a light red patch on the dark dull red of the breadth about it. After another while the leaks along the ridge need plastering: mortar is laid on to stay the inroad of wet, adding a dull white and forming a rough, uncertain undulation along the general drooping curve. Yellow edgings of straw project under the eaves—the work of the sparrows. A cluster of blue-tinted pigeons gathers about the chimney-side; the smoke that comes out of the stack droops and floats sideways, downwards, as if the chimney enjoyed the smother as a man enjoys his pipe. Shattered here and cracked yonder, some missing, some overlapping in curves, the tiles have an aspect of irregular existence. They are not fixed like slates, as it were for ever: they have a newness, and then a middle-age, and a time of decay like human beings.

One roof is not much; but it is often a study. Put a thousand roofs, say rather thousands of red-tiled roofs, and overlook them—not at a great altitude but at a pleasant easy angle—and then you have the groundwork of the first view of London over Bermondsey from the railway. I say groundwork, because the roofs seem the level and surface of the earth, while the glimpses of streets are glimpses of catacombs. A city—as something to look at—depends very much on its roofs. If a city have no character in its roofs it stirs neither heart nor thought. These red-tiled roofs of Bermondsey, stretching away mile upon mile, and brought up at the extremity with thin masts rising above the mist—these red-tiled roofs have a distinctiveness, a character; they are something to think about. Nowhere else is there an entrance to a city like this. The roads by which you approach them give you distant aspects—minarets, perhaps, in the East, domes in Italy; but, coming nearer, the highway somehow plunges into houses, confounding you with façades—and the real place is hidden. Here from the railway you see at once the vastness of London. Roof-tree behind roof-tree, ridge behind ridge, is drawn along in succession, line behind line till they become as close together as the test-lines used for microscopes. Under this surface of roofs what a profundity of life there is! Just as the great horses in the waggons of London streets convey the idea of strength, so the endlessness of the view conveys the idea of a mass of life. Life converges from every quarter. The iron way has many ruts: the rails are its ruts; and by each of these a ceaseless stream of men and women pours over the tiled roofs into London. They come from the populous suburbs, from far-away towns and quiet villages, and from over sea.

Glance down as you pass into the excavations, the streets, beneath the red surface: you catch a glimpse of men and women hastening to and fro, of vehicles, of horses struggling with mighty loads, of groups at the corners, and fragments, as it were, of crowds. Busy life everywhere: no stillness, no quiet, no repose. Life crowded and crushed together; life that has hardly room to live. If the train slackens, look in at the open windows of the houses level with the line—they are always open for air, smoke-laden as it is—and see women and children with scarce room to move, the bed and the dining-table in the same apartment. For they dine and sleep and work and play all at the same time. A man works at night and sleeps by day: he lies yonder as calmly as if in a quiet country cottage. The children have no place to play in but the living-room or the street. It is not squalor—it is crowded life. The people are pushed together by the necessities of existence. These people have no dislike to it at all: it is right enough to them, and so long as business is brisk they are happy. The man who lies sleeping so calmly seems to me to indicate the immensity of the life around more than all the rest. He is oblivious of it all; it does not make him nervous or wakeful; he is so used to it, and bred to it, that it seems to him nothing. When he is awake he does not see it; now he sleeps he does not hear it. It is only in great woods that you cannot see the trees. He is like a leaf in a forest—he is not conscious of it. Long hours of work have given him slumber; and as he sleeps he seems to express by contrast the immensity and endlessness of the life around him.

L

Sometimes a floating haze, now thicker here, and now lit up yonder by the sunshine, brings out objects more distinctly than a clear atmosphere. Away there tall thin masts stand out, rising straight up above the red roofs. There is a faint colour on them; the yards are dark— being inclined, they do not reflect the light at an angle to reach us. Half-furled canvas droops in folds, now swelling a little as the wind blows, now heavily sinking. One white sail is set and gleams alone among the dusky folds; for the canvas at large is dark with coal-dust, with smoke, with the grime that settles everywhere where men labour with bare arms and chests. Still and quiet as trees the masts rise into the hazy air; who would think, merely to look at them, of the endless labour they mean? The labour to load, and the labour to unload; the labour at sea, and the long hours of ploughing the waves by night; the labour at the warehouses; the labour in the fields, the mines, the mountains; the labour in the factories. Ever and again the sunshine gleams now on this group of masts, now on that; for they stand in groups as trees often grow, a thicket here and a thicket yonder. Labour to obtain the material, labour to bring it hither, labour to force it into shape— work without end. Masts are always dreamy to look at: they speak a romance of the sea; of unknown lands; of distant forests aglow with tropical colours and abounding with strange forms of life. In the hearts of most of us there is always a desire for something beyond experience. Hardly any of us but have thought, Some day I will go on a long voyage; but the years go by, and still we have not sailed.

19

After London

I

The Great Forest

THE OLD MEN SAY THEIR FATHERS TOLD THEM THAT soon after the fields were left to themselves a change began to be visible. It became green everywhere in the first spring, after London ended, so that all the country looked alike.

The meadows were green, and so was the rising wheat which had been sown, but which neither had nor would receive any further care. Such arable fields as had not been sown, but where the last stubble had been ploughed up, were overrun with couch-grass, and where the short stubble had not been ploughed, the weeds hid it. So that there was no place which was not more or less green; the footpaths were the greenest of all, for such is the nature of grass where it has once been trodden on, and by-and-by, as the summer came on, the former roads were thickly covered with the grass that had spread out from the margin.

In the autumn, as the meadows were not mown, the grass withered as it stood, falling this way and that, as the wind had blown it; the seeds dropped, and the bennets became a greyish-white, or, where the docks and sorrel were thick, a brownish-red. The wheat, after it had ripened, there being no one to reap it, also remained standing, and was eaten by clouds of sparrows, rooks, and pigeons, which flocked to it and were undisturbed, feasting at their pleasure. As the winter came on, the crops were beaten down by the storms, soaked with the rain, and trodden upon by herds of animals.

Next summer the prostrate straw of the preceding year was concealed by the young green wheat and barley that sprang up from the grain sown by dropping from the ears, and by quantities of docks, thistles, oxeye daisies, and similar plants. This matted mass grew up through the bleached straw. Charlock, too, hid the rotting roots in the fields under a blaze of yellow flower. The young spring meadow-grass could scarcely push its way up through the long dead grass and bennets of the year previous, but docks and thistles, sorrel, wild carrots, and nettles, found no such difficulty.

Footpaths were concealed by the second year, but roads could be traced, though as green as the sward, and were still the best for walking, because the tangled wheat and weeds, and, in the meadows, the long grass, caught the feet of those who tried to pass through. Year by year the original crops of wheat, barley, oats, and beans, asserted their presence by shooting up, but in gradually diminished force, as nettles and coarser plants, such as the wild parsnips, spread out into the fields from the ditches and choked them.

Aquatic grasses from the furrows and water-carriers extended in the meadows, and, with the rushes, helped to destroy or take the place of the former sweet herbage. Meanwhile the brambles, which grew very fast, had pushed forward their prickly runners farther and farther from the hedge till they had now reached ten or fifteen yards. The briars had followed, and the hedges had widened to three or four times their first breadth, the fields being equally contracted. Starting from all sides at once, these brambles and briars in the course of about twenty years met in the centre of the largest fields.

Hawthorn bushes sprang up among them, and, protected by the briars and thorns from grazing animals, the
suckers of elm-trees rose and flourished. Sapling ashes,
oaks, sycamores, and horse-chestnuts, lifted their heads.
Of old time the cattle would have eaten off the seed leaves
with the grass so soon as they were out of the ground, but
now most of the acorns that were dropped by birds, and
the keys that were wafted by the wind, twirling as they
floated, took root and grew into trees. By this time the
brambles and briars had choked up and blocked the
former roads, which were as impassable as the fields.

No fields, indeed, remained, for where the ground was
dry, the thorns, briars, brambles, and saplings already
mentioned filled the space, and these thickets and the
young trees had converted most part of the country into
an immense forest. Where the ground was naturally moist,
and the drains had become choked with willow roots,
which, when confined in tubes, grow into a mass like the
brush of a fox, sedges and flags and rushes covered it.
Thorn bushes were there too, but not so tall; they were
hung with lichen. Besides the flags and reeds, vast quantities of the tallest cow-parsnips or "gicks" rose five or
six feet high, and the willow herb with its stout stem,
almost as woody as a shrub, filled every approach.

By the thirtieth year there was not one single open
place, the hills only excepted, where a man could walk,
unless he followed the tracks of wild creatures or cut
himself a path. The ditches, of course, had long since
become full of leaves and dead branches, so that the water
which should have run off down them stagnated, and
presently spread out into the hollow places and by the
corner of what had once been fields, forming marshes
where the horsetails, flags, and sedges hid the water.

From an elevation, there was nothing visible but endless forest and marsh. On the level ground and plains the view was limited to a short distance, because of the thickets and the saplings which had now become young trees. The downs only were still partially open, yet it was not convenient to walk upon them except in the tracks of animals, because of the long grass which, being no more regularly grazed upon by sheep, as was once the case, grew thick and tangled. Furze, too, and heath covered the slopes, and in places vast quantities of fern. There had always been copses of fir and beech and nut-tree covers, and these increased and spread, while bramble, briar, and hawthorn extended around them.

II

The Lake and the Swamp

At the eastern extremity the Lake narrows, and finally is lost in the vast marshes which cover the site of the ancient London. Through these, no doubt, in the days of the old world there flowed the river Thames. By the changes of the sea level and the sand that was brought up there must have grown up great banks, which obstructed the stream. Vast quantities of timber, the wreckage of towns and bridges, were carried down by the various rivers, and by none more so than by the Thames. These added to the accumulation, which increased the faster because the foundations of the ancient bridges held it like piles driven in for the purpose. And before this the river had become partially choked from the cloacae of the ancient city which poured into it through enormous subterranean aqueducts and drains.

After a time all these shallows and banks became well matted together by the growth of weeds, of willows, and flags, while the tide, ebbing lower at each drawing back, left still more mud and sand. Now it is believed that when this had gone on for a time, the waters of the river, unable to find a channel, began to overflow up into the deserted streets, and especially to fill the underground passages and drains, of which the number and extent was beyond all the power of words to describe. These, by the force of the water, were burst up, and the houses fell in.

For this marvellous city, of which such legends are related, was after all only of brick, and when the ivy grew over and trees and shrubs sprang up, and, lastly, the waters underneath burst in, this huge metropolis was soon overthrown. At this day all those parts which were built upon low ground are marshes and swamps. Those that were upon high ground were, of course, like the other towns, ransacked of all they contained by the remnant that was left; the iron, too, was extracted. Trees growing up by them in course of time cracked the walls, and they fell in. Trees and bushes covered them; ivy and nettles concealed the crumbling masses of brick. . . .

Thus the low-lying parts of the mighty city of London became swamps, and the higher grounds were clad with bushes. The very largest of the buildings fell in, and there was nothing visible but trees and hawthorns on the upper lands, and willows, flags, reeds, and rushes on the lower. These crumbling ruins still more choked the stream, and almost, if not quite, turned it back. If any water ooze past, it is not perceptible, and there is no channel through to the salt ocean. It is a vast stagnant swamp, which no man dare enter, since death would be his inevitable fate.

There exhales from this oozy mass so fatal a vapour that no animal can endure it. The black water bears a greenish-brown floating scum, which for ever bubbles up from the putrid mud of the bottom. When the wind collects the miasma, and, as it were, presses it together, it becomes visible as a low cloud which hangs over the place. The cloud does not advance beyond the limit of the marsh, seeming to stay there by some constant attraction; and well it is for us that it does not, since at such times when the vapour is thickest, the very wild-fowl leave the reeds, and fly from the poison. There are no fishes, neither can eels exist in the mud, nor even newts. It is dead.

The flags and reeds are coated with slime and noisome to the touch; there is one place where even these do not grow, and where there is nothing but an oily liquid, green and rank. It is plain there are no fishes in the water, for herons do not go thither, nor the kingfishers, not one of which approaches the spot. They say the sun is sometimes hidden by the vapour when it is thickest, but I do not see how any can tell this, since they could not enter the cloud, as to breathe it when collected by the wind is immediately fatal. For all the rottenness of a thousand years and of many hundred millions of human beings is there festering under the stagnant water, which has sunk down into and penetrated the earth, and floated up to the surface the contents of the buried cloacae.

Many scores of men have, I fear, perished in the attempt to enter this fearful place, carried on by their desire of gain. For it can scarcely be disputed that untold treasure lies hidden therein, but guarded by terrors greater than fiery serpents. These have usually made their endeavours to enter in severe and continued frost, or in the height of a drought. Frost diminishes the power of the vapour, and the marshes can then, too, be partially traversed, for there is no channel for a boat. But the moment anything be moved, whether it be a bush, or a willow, even a flag, if the ice be broken, the pestilence rises yet stronger. Besides which, there are portions which never freeze, and which may be approached unawares, or a turn of the wind may drift the gas towards the explorer.

In the midst of the summer, after long heat, the vapour rises, and is in a degree dissipated into the sky, and then by following devious ways an entrance may be effected, but always at the cost of illness. If the explorer be unable to quit the spot before night, whether in summer or winter, his death is certain. In the earlier times some bold and adventurous men did indeed succeed in getting a few jewels, but since then the marsh has become more dangerous, and its pestilent character, indeed, increases year by year, as the stagnant water penetrates deeper. So that now for very many years no such attempts have been made. . . .

Towards the Lake the sand thrown up by the waves has long since formed a partial barrier between the sweet water and the stagnant, rising up to within a few feet of the surface. This barrier is overgrown with flags and reeds, where it is shallow. Here it is possible to sail along the sweet water within an arrow-shot of the swamp. Nor, indeed, would the stagnant mingle with the sweet, as is evident at other parts of the swamp, where streams flow side by side with the dark or reddish water; and there are pools, upon one side of which the deer drink, while the other is not frequented even by rats.

The common people aver that demons reside in these swamps; and, indeed, at night fiery shapes are seen, which, to the ignorant, are sufficient confirmation of such tales. The vapour, where it is most dense, takes fire, like the blue flame of spirits, and these flaming clouds float to and fro, and yet do not burn the reeds. The superstitious trace in them the forms of demons and winged fiery serpents, and say that white spectres haunt the margin of the marsh after dusk. In a lesser degree, the same thing has taken place with other ancient cities. It is true that there are not always swamps, but the sites are uninhabitable because of the emanations from the ruins. Therefore they are avoided. Even the spot where a single house has been known to have existed, is avoided by the hunters in the woods.

They say when they are stricken with ague or fever, that they must have unwittingly slept on the site of an ancient habitation. Nor can the ground be cultivated near the ancient towns, because it causes fever; and thus it is that the present places of the same name are often miles distant from the former locality. No sooner does the plough or the spade turn up an ancient site than those who work there are attacked with illness. And thus the cities of the old world, and their houses and habitations are deserted and lost in the forest.

III

The Site of London

The thought struck Felix that perhaps he might find a spring somewhere in the island, and he started at once up over the hill. At the top he paused. The sun had not sunk, but had disappeared as a disk. In its place was a billow of blood, for so it looked, a vast up-heaved billow of glowing blood surging on the horizon. Over it flickered a tint of palest blue, like that seen in fire. The black waters, reflected the glow, and the yellow vapour around was suffused with it. Though momentarily startled, Felix did not much heed these appearances; he was still dazed and heavy from his sleep.

He went on, looking for a spring, sometimes walking on firm ground, sometimes sinking to the ankle in a friable solid like black sand. The ground looked, indeed, as if it had been burnt, but there were no charred stumps of timber such as he had seen on the sites of forest fires. The extreme dreariness seemed to oppress his spirits, and he went on and on in a heavy waking dream. Descending into a plain, he lost sight of the flaming sunset and the black waters. In the level plain the desolation was yet more marked; there was not a grass blade or plant; the surface was hard, black, and burned, resembling iron, and indeed in places it resounded to his feet, though he supposed that was the echo from hollow passages beneath.

Several times he shook himself, straightened himself up, and endeavoured to throw off the sense of drowsy weight which increased upon him. He could not do so; he walked with bent back, and crept, as it were, over the iron land which radiated heat. A shimmer like that of water appeared in front; he quickened his pace, but could not get to it, and he realized presently that it was a mirage which receded as he advanced. There was no pleasant summer twilight; the sunset was succeeded by an indefinite gloom, and while this shadow hung overhead the yellow vapour around was faintly radiant. Felix suddenly stopped, having stepped, as he thought, on a skeleton.

Another glance, however, showed that it was merely the impression of one, the actual bones had long since disappeared. The ribs, the skull, and limbs were drawn on the black ground in white lines as if it had been done with a broad piece of chalk. Close by he found three or four more, intertangled and superimposed as if the unhappy beings had fallen partly across each other, and in that position had mouldered away leaving nothing but their outline. From among a variety of objects that were scattered about Felix picked up something that shone; it was a diamond bracelet of one large stone, and a small square of blue china-tile with a curious heraldic animal drawn on it. Evidently these had belonged to one or other of the party who had perished.

Though startled at the first sight, it was curious that Felix felt so little horror; the idea did not occur to him that he was in danger as these had been. Inhaling the gaseous emanations from the soil and contained in the yellow vapour, he had become narcotized, and moved as if under the influence of opium, while wide awake, and capable of rational conduct. His senses were deadened, and did not carry the usual vivid impression to the mind; he saw things as if they were afar off. Accidentally looking back, he found that his footmarks, as far as he could see, shone with a phosphoric light like that of "touchwood" in the dark. Near at hand they did not shine; the appearance did not come till some minutes had elapsed. His track was visible behind till the vapour hid it. As the evening drew on the vapour became more luminous, and somewhat resembled an aurora.

Still anxious for water he proceeded as straight ahead as he could, and shortly became conscious of an indefinite cloud which kept pace with him on either side. When he turned to look at either of the clouds, the one looked at disappeared. It was not condensed enough to be visible to direct vision, yet he was aware of it from the corner of his eye. Shapeless and threatening, the gloomy thickness of the air floated beside him like the vague monster of a dream. Sometimes he fancied that he saw an arm or a limb among the folds of the cloud, or an approach to a face; the instant he looked it vanished. Marching at each hand these vapours bore him horrible company.

His brain became unsteady, and flickering things moved about him; yet, though alarmed, he was not afraid; his senses were not acute enough for fear. The heat increased, his hands were intolerably hot as if he had been in a fever, he panted, but did not perspire. A dry heat like an oven burned his blood in his veins. His head felt enlarged, and his eyes seemed alight; he could see these two globes of phosphoric light under his brows. They seemed to stand out so that he could see them. He thought his path straight, it was really curved; nor did he know that he staggered as he walked.

Presently a white object appeared ahead; and on coming to it, he found it was a wall, white as snow, with some kind of crystal. He touched it, when the wall fell immediately with a crushing sound as if pulverized, and disappeared in a vast cavern at his feet. Beyond this chasm he came to more walls like those of houses, such as would be left if the roofs fell in. He carefully avoided touching them, for they seemed as brittle as glass, and merely a white powder having no consistency at all. As he advanced these remnants of buildings increased in number, so that he had to wind in and out and round them. In some places the crystallized wall had fallen of itself, and he could see down into the cavern; for the house had either been built partly underground, or, which was more probable, the ground had risen. Whether the walls had been of bricks or stone or other material he could not tell; they were now like salt.

Soon wearying of winding round these walls, Felix returned and retraced his steps until he was outside the place, and then went on towards the left. Not long after, as he still walked in a dream and without feeling his feet, he descended a slight slope and found the ground change in colour from black to a dull red. In his dazed state he had taken several steps out into this red before he noticed that it was liquid, unctuous and slimy, like a thick oil. It deepened rapidly and was already over his shoes; he returned to the black shore and stood looking out over the water, if such it could be called.

The luminous yellow vapour had now risen a height of ten or fifteen feet, and formed a roof both over the land and over the red water, under which it was possible to see for a great distance. The surface of the red oil or viscid liquid was perfectly smooth, and, indeed, it did not seem as if any wind could rouse a wave on it, much less that a swell should be left after the gale had gone down. Disappointed in his search for water to drink, Felix mechanically turned to go back.

He followed his luminous footmarks, which he could see a long way before him. His trail curved so much that he made many short cuts across the winding line he had left. His weariness was now so intense that all feeling had departed. His feet, his limbs, and hands were numbed. The subtle poison of the emanations from the earth had begun to deaden his nerves. It seemed a full hour or more to him till he reached the spot where the skeletons were drawn in white upon the ground.

He passed a few yards to one side of them, and stumbled over a heap of something which he did not observe, as it was black like the level ground. It emitted a metallic sound, and looking he saw that he had kicked his foot against a great heap of money. The coins were black as ink; he picked up a handful and went on. Hitherto Felix had accepted all that he saw as something so strange as to be unaccountable. During his advance into this region in the canoe he had in fact become slowly stupefied by the poisonous vapour he had inhaled. His mind was partly in abeyance; it acted, but only after some time had elapsed. He now at last began to realize his position; the finding of the heap of blackened money touched a chord of memory. These skeletons were the miserable relics of men who had ventured, in search of ancient treasures, into the deadly marshes over the site of the mightiest city of former days. The deserted and utterly extinct city of London was under his feet. . . . The earth on which he walked, the black earth, leaving phosphoric footmarks behind him, was composed of the mouldered bodies of millions of men who had passed away in the centuries during which the city existed. He shuddered as he moved; he hastened, yet could not go fast, his numbed limbs would not permit him.

Notes

1. *London Overture.* "Footpaths," "Nature near London."

2. *The Story of My Heart.* Jefferies was much in advance of the thought of his own time. A lonely and independent thinker, he went his way unaffected by the changing currents of taste. Like Ruskin before him in "Unto This Last", Jefferies saw clearly the evil of current economics and the folly of those who believed poverty and vice sent by Heaven. He knew them man-made and that they could be removed by wise and far-sighted planning. But equally he would not neglect the soul of man. In another place he says: "My sympathies and hopes are with the light of the future, only I should like it to come from Nature. The clock should be read by the sunshine, not the sun timed by the clock."

3. *The Lions in Trafalgar Square.* "Toilers of the Field." This is a comparatively prentice essay, although a very charming one, in Jefferies' early manner. He was, however, as many examples in later writing were to prove, much interested in statuary, which at its best, as he notes in "Nature at the Louvre", he thought "the beautiful made tangible in human form". There are also several significant passages on this point in "The Story of My Heart". Since Jefferies' day the reproach he levels at the absence of fine works of art in the open air no longer holds good.

The Lions on the radial pedestals at the foot of the Nelson Column were provided for in Railton's original design. They were to be carved in granite, and a provisional commission for the work was given to the sculptor, J. G. Lough, by the original committee. In 1846 Lough, after consultation with Railton, wrote to the Department declining the commission on the ground that the lions were all alike and might as well be sphinxes; they were purely "architectonic", and he would not willingly involve his professional reputation in such a work under Railton's restrictions.

The proposal to provide lions made no progress until, in 1858, Landseer was commissioned to produce designs.

It is interesting to learn, in view of the controversial speculations and assertions, that Landseer's designs for the legs may have been influenced by the fact that he made use of what the departmental records call the "anatomical lion" at Turin, the property of the then King of Sardinia. Plaster casts were taken and sent to Landseer to assist him in his work. The models of the lions were approved in 1863 and the castings were undertaken by Marochetti. The Lions were completed and fitted on their pedestals in 1867. Landseer received £6,000 and Marochetti £11,000 for their services.

P. 40. 4. *Sky over London.* "Magpie Fields," "Nature near London." Jefferies constantly watched and noted skies. Many admirable and eloquent passages in his writings testify to this.

P. 45. 5. *Sunlight in a London Square.* "The Life of the Fields." In the manner of the later imaginative and poetic essays, and among the very finest he ever composed. In one of Jefferies' letters he wrote to a friend: "Some people have the idea that my knowledge is confined to the fields; as a matter of fact, I have had quite as much to do with London—all parts of it, too—and am very fond of what I may call a thickness of the people such as exists there. I like the solitude of the hills, and the hum of the most crowded city: I dislike little towns and villages. I dream in London quite as much as in the woodlands. It's a wonderful place to dream in." My friend H. S. Salt, who quotes from this letter, adds the comment: "Compare Thoreau's letter to Emerson from New York, May 23, 1843. 'There are two things I hear, and am aware I live in the neighbourhood of—the roar of the sea and the hum of the city.'"

This was probably a mood at times, but his heart, say what he would, was more constantly in the fields and on the downs and by the sea. I illustrate this by the following quotation from one of his note-books in my possession: "All I cared for and desired was the fields, the hills, the sea, the coast. I had no desire to make money or excel in anything, or fame."

M

P. 50.   6. *Nature near London*. From the Preface. Most of the Essays in this book were written at Surbiton.

P. 53.   7. *A Wet Night in London*. "The Open Air." A most charming and effective period piece.

P. 59.   8. *The Pigeons at the British Museum*. "The Life of the Fields." "Seats should be placed here, under the great columns or by the grass, so that one might enjoy the sunshine after books and watch the pigeons." Seats *were* placed under the columns many years ago, and trees were planted on the grass a year or two before the war, but both have had to be removed for the duration. While the editor in his earlier days was eating his lunch, the sight of the late Sir Wallis Budge feeding the pigeons on the lawn outside the British Museum is a very vivid memory.

P. 64.   9. *Fleet Street*. "Amaryllis at the Fair." This is Jefferies' most successful novel. The pages quoted are another very delightful period piece. Alere Flamma was drawn from Fred Gyde, brother of Mrs. Jefferies. He was an engraver and a printer. Edward Thomas thinks of "Amaryllis at the Fair" as "a complete, expressive book, full of Jefferies himself and of the world as he saw it."

P. 73.   10. *Trees about Town*. "Nature near London." This essay is a good example of Jefferies' descriptive manner, where he is more or less writing up from his note-books what he had seen on his walks abroad, in the woods, the fields and the town. It is placed in his middle period, very informative but lacking the highest side of his talent. None the less, it is very pleasant and many readers who miss the deeper spiritual power of the later essays may find refreshment and pleasure here.

P. 82.   11. *Flocks of Birds*. "Nature near London."

P. 90.   12. *A London Trout*. "Nature near London." This charming study, with its companion, "The Brook", also to be found in "Nature near London", but not quoted, was written at Surbiton. The stream was the Hogsmill Brook. Here he was no longer the sportsman, but the artist and humanitarian.

P. 100. 13. *The Coming of Summer.* "Toilers of the Field." This pleasantly descriptive and colourful essay was published posthumously, first in *Longman's Magazine,* December, 1891, and then collected in "Toilers of the Field", in the following year. Passages from this essay Jefferies had already included in *Round About a London Copse,* 1883.

P. 114. 14. *Herbs.* "Nature near London." A finished essay indeed, which is very attractive in the way it conveys instruction with pleasure in the writing itself. Part of the charm indeed is to be found in "the informative gossip" of the open air, of which Jefferies is the master, often imitated but never surpassed.

P. 124. 15. *The Modern Thames.* "The Open Air." Compare the essay, *The River. Nature Near London.*

P. 147. 16. *On the London Road.* "The Open Air." The leery Londoner may be compared with Jefferies' general dislike of the more unpleasant and tiresome human species in "The Bathing Season", also in "The Open Air". Like every man of private judgment and independent mind, Jefferies hated the mob spirit and the common degradation of the dreg type, just as he detested the scum at the top. He loved the manly, thoughtful, active citizen, who goes on his way, duly interested in the welfare of his country and countrymen, but not too anxious to interfere unduly with the rights or happiness of others.

P. 153. 17. *Venice in the East End.* "The Life of the Fields."

P. 159. 18. *Red Roofs of London.* "The Open Air." Compare "Nature on the Roof", to be found in the same book. "The years go by, and still we have not sailed." How true it is of other things than an actual voyage! How many can say with Shelley:

> *My spirit's bark is driven, far from the shore,*
> *Far from the trembling throng, whose sails were never to the*
> *tempest given?*

P. 163. 19. *After London.* "After London; or, Wild England."
Jefferies wrote to his friend and publisher Mr. C. J.
Longman in June, 1885, about "After London" and
said:

> "It is in no sense a novel, more like a romance, but
> a romance of a *real* character. You will, I think, do me
> the justice to say that it is original."

"The Relapse into Barbarism", the first part of the book,
from which our extracts are taken, is a masterly piece of
writing.

"After London" has some autobiography in it. Felix is
Jefferies himself, and Oliver is his brother.

The following very pertinent and interesting description of Richard
Jefferies may be given. It is quoted from Sir Walter Besant's sym-
pathetic and early appreciation, "The Eulogy of Richard Jefferies"
(1888):

"In appearance Richard Jefferies was very tall—over six feet. He
was always thin. His hair was dark brown; his beard was brown,
with a shade of auburn; his forehead both high and broad; his features
strongly marked; his nose long, clear, and straight; his lower lip thick;
his eyebrows distinguished by a meditative droop; his complexion
was fair, with very little colour. The most remarkable feature in his
face was his large and clear blue eye; it was so full that it ought to
have been short-sighted, yet his sight was far as well as keen. His
face was full of thought; he walked with somewhat noiseless tread.
He never carried an umbrella or wore a greatcoat, nor, except in
very cold weather, did he wear gloves. He had great powers of
endurance in walking, but his physical strength was never great.
In manner, he was always reserved; at times so much so as to appear
morose to those who knew him but slightly. He made few friends."

Besant also gives the following details of Jefferies' personal habits,
and this refers more especially to his period of residence at Surbiton:

"As for his personal habits, Jefferies was extremely simple and
regular, even methodical. He breakfasted always at eight o'clock,
often on nothing but dry toast and tea. After breakfast he went to
his study, where he remained writing until half-past eleven. At that
hour he always went out, whatever the weather and in all seasons,
and walked until one o'clock. This morning walk was an absolute

necessity for him. At one o'clock he returned and took an early dinner, which was his only substantial meal. His tastes were simple. He liked to have a plain roast or boiled joint, with abundance of vegetables, of which he was very fond, especially asparagus, sea-kale, and mushrooms. He would have preferred ale, but he found that light claret or burgundy suited him better, and therefore he drank daily a little of one or the other.

"Dinner over, he read his daily paper, and slept for an hour by the fireside. At three o'clock he awoke, and went for another walk, coming home at half-past four. He thus walked for three hours every day, which, for a quick walker, gives a distance of twelve miles —a very good allowance of fresh air. Jefferies acquired the habit of noting down in his walks, and storing away, those thousands of little things which make his writings the despair of those people who think themselves minute observers. He took tea at five, and then worked again in his study till half-past eight, when he commonly finished work for the day. . . . He took a little supper at nine, of cold meat and bread, with a glass of claret, and then read or conversed until eleven, when he went to bed. He talked with most eagerness on the Labour Question. He took tobacco very rarely. . . .

"He had not a large library, because the books which he most wished to procure were beyond his means. His favourite novelists were Scott and Charles Reade. He also liked the works of Ouida and Miss Braddon. He never cared greatly for Charles Dickens. He was never tired of Goethe's "Faust", which was always new to him. He loved old ballads, and among the poets, Dryden's works were his favourite reading. *In one thing he was imperious: the house must be kept quiet—absolutely quiet—while he was at work.* Any household operations that made the least noise had to be postponed till he went out for his walk. . . . He carried a note-book always with him on his walks, and while he was always watching the infinite wealth and variety of Nature, the multitudinous forms of life, he was always noting down what he saw. To read these note-books is like reading an unclassified index to the works of nature. They prove—if that wanted any proof—how careful he was to set down nothing that had not been noted and proved by himself."

On Jefferies' death, there were twenty-two of these note-books in all, of which seven have been lost, all trace having vanished. All twenty-two were in the possession of Sir Walter Besant, when he wrote his study of Jefferies, and Edward Thomas also consulted them for the full length biography. The fifteen surviving note-books are part of the Jefferies' collection of the present editor.

Very few people survive who knew Jefferies in the flesh. C. P. Scott of the *Manchester Guardian* and C. J. Longman of Longmans, Green, two of his staunchest friends, and to whom most of his letters were addressed, are both dead. Besant, who wrote about him with much insight, never actually met Jefferies. J. W. North, the landscape artist, who illustrated one or two of his articles, including "Summer in Somerset", "English Illustrated Magazine" (1887), and who was one of of his few intimate friends of later days, contributed some memories to Besant's book. But he, too, has long since passed. I only knew one man who had actually seen Richard Jefferies, Spencer, the famous second-hand bookseller of Oxford Street, opposite Mudie's, who died several years ago. He was specially interested in Jefferies' first editions. My own Jefferies collection is fairly complete; besides the fifteen note-books mentioned above, it includes various autograph letters, copies of most of his first editions, with the exception of one or two of the practically unprocurable early pamphlets, and several manuscripts, both published and unpublished. I have had much interesting correspondence with Jefferies' only daughter, Mrs. Phyllis Hargrave, and with his son, the late Richard Harold Jefferies.

The Chief Works of Richard Jefferies

The Scarlet Shawl, A Novel, 1874.

Restless Human Hearts, A Novel, 3 vols., 1875.

World's End, A Story in Three Books, 3 vols., 1877.

The Gamekeeper at Home; Or, Sketches of Natural History and Rural Life, 1878, Illustrated Edition by Charles Whymper, 1880.

Wild Life in a Southern County, 1879.

The Amateur Poacher, 1879.

Greene Ferne Farm, 1880.

Hodge and His Masters, 2 vols., 1880.

Round About a Great Estate, 1880.

Wood Magic; A Fable, 1881.

Bevis: The Story of a Boy, 1882.

Nature near London, 1883.

The Story of My Heart: My Autobiography, 1883.

Red Deer, 1884.

The Life of the Fields, 1884.

The Dewy Morn, A Novel, 2 vols., 1884.

After London: Or, Wild England, 1885.

The Open Air, 1885.

Amaryllis at the Fair, A Novel, 1887.

Posthumous.

Field and Hedgerow; Being the Last Essays of Richard Jefferies, Collected by His Widow, 1889.

The Toilers of the Field, 1892.

The Hills and the Vale, with an Introduction by Edward Thomas, 1909.

Richard Jefferies also wrote and published, between 1873–1876, several pamphlets, which are now exceedingly scarce. They include

"Reporting, Editing and Authorship", 1873, "A Memoir of the Goddards of North Wilts", 1873, "Jack Brass", 1873, and "Suez-cide", 1876.

The first three novels are of little value, but with the publication of "Greene Ferne Farm", in 1880, Jefferies' fiction showed a great advance in power and freshness of natural vision. "The Dewy Morn" and "Amaryllis at the Fair" are full of the most delightful nature pictures, and both Felise and Amaryllis respectively, the heroines, are painted with compelling artistry and local colour as children of Nature. There are some autobiographical touches in both books.

The following works may be consulted:

The Eulogy of Richard Jefferies, by Sir Walter Besant, 1888.

Nature in Books, Some Studies in Biography, by P. Anderson Graham, 1891.

Richard Jefferies, A Study, by H. S. Salt, 1894.

Passages from the Nature Writings of Richard Jefferies, by A. H. Hyatt, 1905.

Richard Jefferies, His Life and Work, by Edward Thomas, 1909.

Richard Jefferies, by Reginald Arkell, 1933.

Out-of-Doors with Richard Jefferies, edited by Eric Fitch Daglish.

Jefferies' England, edited by Samuel J. Looker, 1937; second edition, 1943.

Readings from Richard Jefferies, made by Ronald Hook, 1940. (This book is specially excellent for beginners in the study of Jefferies and the notes are valuable.)

The Unpublished Diaries and Note-books of Richard Jefferies, with an Essay, "A Tangle of Autumn", edited from manuscripts in his possession by Samuel J. Looker, 1941.

Jefferies' Countryside, edited by Samuel J. Looker, 1944.